AN APOLOGY FOR OLD MAIDS

AN APOLOGY FOR OLD MAIDS

AND OTHER ESSAYS

BY

HENRY DWIGHT SEDGWICK

WITH A PREFACE BY
OWEN WISTER

Essay Index Reprint Series

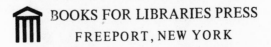

BOOKS FOR LIBRARIES PRESS
FREEPORT, NEW YORK

First Published 1916
Reprinted 1968

LIBRARY OF CONGRESS CATALOG CARD NUMBER:
68-8492

PRINTED IN THE UNITED STATES OF AMERICA

TO

THE CLASS OF 1916

OF

THE BREARLEY SCHOOL

THIS VOLUME IS AFFECTIONATELY

DEDICATED

" Retire into thyself."
MARCUS AURELIUS.

All the essays in this volume appeared in the *Atlantic Monthly*, except "An Apology for Old Maids" which appeared in the *Yale Review*. For permission to republish them here I am indebted to the kindness of the Editors of those reviews.

H. D. S.

New York, 1916.

TABLE OF CONTENTS

PREFACE

ONLY a few hours ago I paused at a teeming book-stall in the South Station, Boston. Beside me stood Inelegant Leisure in petticoats, choosing. The emotion that rose in me was one of thankfulness that a paper famine is said to be upon us.

Lot was assured that a given number of respectable citizens could avert from his town its doom. Had we, I wondered, among our huge population of novelists enough for salvation ? — Well, I thought next, among another company it's more hopeful. A small company, to be sure, and they don't live in the best-seller belt ; but, any how, they do live — and persist.

Why is it that our American essayists are on the whole so good and our American novelists are on the whole so bad ? As with guns so with books it is the man behind them that counts. He matters ; more than his talent, or his learning, or his subject, more than anything, he matters. It is Montaigne himself we enjoy ; it is Scott himself, Scott the man throughout his romances, who lives most, who fills and warms their pages with his noble, kind wholesomeness. A novel taps its author's intimate essence just as searchingly as any essay, is as much a vehicle for interpretation and comment (visible or invisible), and the pose of impersonality adopted by certain French writers deceives not this generation and never need have deceived any. Inevitably the man flows into his book, and if he is a vacuum the book will be empty — and so back we come to our question again : why do our essays mostly size up so well while our stories size up mostly so ill ? Pick up the first, you find a somebody behind them generally, behind the last generally a nobody. But why ?

Do these writing nobodys fancy a real novel an easy thing to make, or merely that a quack novel is an easy thing to sell ? Is Inelegant Leisure in petticoats the sole root of the evil ? It is to be noticed at our railroad-stalls that the fresh work of fiction has come to bear a startling resemblance to the box of fresh candy beside it, and that over both Inelegant Leisure seems to hover impartially on her way to her week-ends.

The question is worth an essay. Let some one of that good company deal with it and tell us how it comes about that most of our essayists have from the early days even until the present written all round most of our novelists ; that Irving in his kind is better than Cooper in his kind ; that Emerson is better than Hawthorne ; that "The Autocrat of the Breakfast-table" has more life in it than

"Elsie Venner"; that Poe's critical writing is more remarkable (for that time of day) than his tales, which Tieck and Hoffmann obviously prompted; and that our two most famous pieces of American prose belong, both of them, in their essence, to the family of the essay — Washington's Farewell Address, and Lincoln's Speech at Gettysburg.

I merely look the present ground over, glance at our bursting shelf of fiction, compare it to our decent shelf of essays, observe the railroad book-stalls and Inelegant Leisure in petticoats, survey the best-seller belt — and offer my American thanks to our American essayists for saving our face.

Yes; that is indeed what they do; they save our face. We can point to them without blushing. Amid the weltering inanity of present American Letters it is their pens chiefly that write the leavening sentences of wit, thought, and cultivation, it is their books mainly that we send to friends in the civilized world, because they show that all of us do not live in the best-seller belt, that some of us are writers and readers with civilized intelligence. Our gratitude to them is kin to that which we feel towards any and every American who through word or deed has helped the Allies. They are our vindicators.

In the track of Mr. Sedgwick's first volume of essays this also shall voyage for our vindication. He has built here, as it were, a quiet house of revery. In it, as you

wander about among the various rooms, you seem to hear
the sound of an organ somewhere, patches of light from
old stained glass seem to fall on certain spots, and not
a noise from the street enters. At one of the windows,
indeed, the War looks in : but the War is no noise from
the street ; through it speaks the voice of our stricken
planet. In Mr. Sedgwick's pages the "incantations of
hope" — I borrow a word from one of them — are subdued to mingle with many other strains. I have found
no better reply to Emerson's fallacy that a translation is
as good as the original than a paragraph of Mr. Sedgwick's. I cannot be as sure as he is that Goethe's influence upon us was once so potent — but the author has
reflected about this and I have not. Indeed, the point
is not that you agree or disagree with Mr. Sedgwick
about Old Age and Youth, or can derive simultaneous
comforts from reason and mysticism : the house is full
of tender beauty and ministers like the quiet *Andante* of
some symphony to the spirit's well-being.

OWEN WISTER.

October 19, 1916.

AN APOLOGY FOR OLD MAIDS

AN APOLOGY FOR OLD MAIDS

MARRIED people, animated by the prejudices of an animal ancestry and by a jealous *esprit de corps*, long ago created a legend about celibates, which depicts them as crotchety, graceless, ill-dressed, ill-mannered, ugly, and selfish; and they have taught this legend to so many generations of children that even now little boys look on celibates with disdain. And, as little boys grow to be bigger boys, disdain gains support from a vague knowledge that if celibates had succeeded in winning the world over to their horrid way of thinking, they, princes of the kingdom of youth, would never have come into their own at all. This silly legend has also been taken up by thoughtless jesters, who ridicule that group of celibates least able to defend themselves, elderly women; and their mockery encourages boys in the gross illusion. But the legend gives way before a widening experience; and the high idealism that

impels celibates to take their solitary way must
always, sooner or later, make itself known by
its fruits.

Who, that looks back on the steadily deepening,
steadily refining, memories of the past, does not
see some celibate figure that shone on his path
with a peculiar light? Ordinarily such figures
are the figures of women, for the deprivation of
motherhood is a greater loss to a woman than the
deprivation of paternity to a man, and renders
her more fit to pour into an alien channel her
dammed-up sympathies; but it is not always so
— the celibate brother, uncle, or priest, may fill
as large a space in the gracious retrospect of
memory for a girl as the unmarried woman for a
boy. The child across whose path the light
from that figure fell could not analyze those
qualities of which he was aware in the spinster,
but he soon learned to recognize them, to enjoy
them, to love them, to need them. In her company, free from the spirit of the household, un-
vexed by the genius of the family, he wandered
into a pleasant, unfenced spaciousness, where his
individuality found a liberal reception, where his
tastes and whims received each a separate and
personal welcome. Perhaps the radiant figure
was an aunt or elderly cousin, bearing on her

face the show of solitary communions, who, at his call, wrapping her shoulders in a white shawl would walk beside him in a tolerant yet restraining sympathy, as if she beheld what he did "with larger, other eyes than" his, and suggested appreciations here and there quite different from family appreciations. She did not take away from his interest or pleasure in the family household, but controlled and encouraged those moods, those closed compartments of a boy's life into which a family has no admittance; she was the compassionate goddess of solitude, of melancholy, of those vague affections that in the period of adolescence grow into religion or love, and spend themselves in moody wanderings through fields and woods, in bad verses, in indignant outbursts at the commonness, the vulgarity of life. She was not called upon to reconcile those fitful periods with due regard for the dinner hour, for company, for lessons, for the social duties of croquet or tennis; she did not repeat the inadequate formulas of tutorial and domestic life; she did not have to enforce rules based on the greatest good of the greatest number of children; she left unopened those budgets of good advice, which each generation solemnly receives from the generation before, and passes on solemnly to the generation after. She stood apart as the friend of his individuality, of his foolish fancies, of his conceits and wayward desires, of his boyish admirations and hopes, of his incapacities for dealing with the ordinary life about him.

Perhaps that graceful and radiant figure, which to the inefficient boy appeared the embodiment of wisdom and sweet reason, had cast at her, behind her back, from some careless lips, the epithet "old maid." The coarse monosyllables fell with a thud on his indignant ear. The irreverence packed into that term was only comparable to indifference to a moonlit night, to Shelley, to the arched pine walk, to the violin. The scoff, whether intended as such or not, was the first thing to set him wondering as to the differences between that beloved figure and other figures also beloved, and to offer the clue that led to the explanation of those differences. Was it because she was an old maid, that she shed so fresh an atmosphere around her, like an unseen spring cooling and quickening a mossy spot; that she stood between the common conventional course of daily family life and the impatient demands of adolescent moods; that she applied her comprehensive yet unobtrusive criticism to the standards of what he called the world; that she could comfort so effectively hurts that others unwittingly gave, and sympathize with the virtue mingled and blended with his faults? Was that the reason that she cheered and encouraged the lonely little boy by asserting the value of his individual soul? Were such the consequences of childlessness, of perpetual maidenhood? Then why did those boys and girls, who embodied his world and had no inkling of his fitful moods, call her "old maid" in derision?

The phrase "old maid," to which the mating instincts have grudged the gentleness and refinement of polysyllables, conjures up a vision of outer isolation, which to the uncelibate looks cold and dismal. A ghostly atmosphere envelops that limbo beyond the hearth, outside the home; and the lonely women wandering there wear a sad livery. Are we deceived by the imagination, or by the flickering light cast by the ruddy fire of our hearths; or is the veiled melancholy, that as children we saw and did not understand yet found so sympathetic to our discontents, a sign that nature has punished the violation of her law? Nature, goddess of instinct, stern, as she needs must be in order to be kind, compels obedience by what means she can; and upon those that disobey she sets the stamp of her displeasure. At her bidding, corporeal existence rebels against final extinction.

Backward it looks, and through the sequent generations, human and prehuman, back through the vastness of unrecorded time, all along in uninterrupted illumination, it sees the cheerful glow of life, the radiance of the sacred fire, flaming, gleaming, glimmering, without a break, back to the first Promethean spark that glittered in the lifeless world; turning forward, it beholds the dark come again in all the repulsiveness of cold, dead vacancy. The poor warm body, rejoicing in the sun, shudders in corporeal trepidation; it cannot escape the self-reproach of treason, that it has suffered the sacred fire, — tended, cherished, preserved, with such great pains, at such great cost, fed upon love, devotion, and self-denial, — to die out. No living thing can betray the confidence of nature without remorse; and that mute self-condemnation, in spite of the persuasions of conscience or the bravado of reason, leaves its ineffaceable mark.

Nor is this consciousness of treason her only punishment. The old maid bars against herself the single gate that leads into the Kingdom of Heaven of this world; she shall never have possession of those

> Stragglers into loving arms
> Those climbers up of knees

that constitute for fathers and mothers the revelation and proof of a divine element in humanity;
she shall never see incarnate in big round eyes and
baby fingers the innocence, the love, the faith,
the fearlessness, of that Kingdom of Heaven.

The celibate is brave, and what seems to us a
distinguishing mark of inward pain, may be in
part the grimness of a resolute courage. In days
gone by, old maids were strong in the belief of
an immortal soul. Upborne by an exalted mood,
they rebuked the body, and looked forward to
the rapturous union of Being with Being. Now
that the spirit apart from the body is less easily
perceived, the celibate has the greater need of
courage; to defy nature, in spite of religious dis-
belief, solely for the sake of an ideal, for the sake
of spiritual salvation during the brief period of
bodily life, has a touch of the heroic. For nature
is no mean enemy; she does not turn and run before a sudden onslaught of spiritual frenzy. Nature can wait; this is the source of her power.
Individuals upon individuals, generations upon
generations, may rebel against her laws; she
abides and punishes the disobedient. She abides,
and in the course of time the wilfulness of her children spends itself, their passion for things of the
spirit droops, and they return, "like colts that

have frisked for a day in the fields," back to their stalls and obedience at night. Only a steadfast courage, a steadfast faith, in the daily, hourly, momentary, worth of the spirit continues to hold out. The solitary old maid who has turned her back upon the comforts of affection, of sympathy, of a home, of children, of comradeship in passing through the great dark of this existence, in which like children we need to hold one another's hands to keep our courage up, may not to the careless eye present a conspicuous figure of heroism, but perhaps the ideal has no more valiant champion than she.

Though from one point of view the old maid's struggle for her own spiritual salvation may seem to be a matter of no special concern to general human society, yet from another it is of much concern, for she can render society services of great and peculiar importance. Her opportunities call for her; her uses make her a necessary supplement to the mother in all the tasks laid on women, other than the primary task of maternity.

The mother is a passionate partisan, she is all for nature. Whatever her maternal feelings suggest becomes her duty, her creed, her truth. She sacrifices herself for her children, she is ready to sacrifice all things else for them; she is a fanatic in the cause of animal immortality and prostrates herself in blind adoration before the god of earthly life. Her judgments are all crooked, for she bases all her opinions upon the law of maternity, as a lawyer bases his on the Constitution. The maternal instinct, so strong emotionally, so weak rationally, bursts into intemperate theories. She values no principle but that of animal life, she knows no measure but that of numbers. Quantity! Quantity! is the mother's cry.

To the old spinster, safe at anchor out of the hot current of corporeal existence, the quality of life is of more consequence than its quantity — though more life is good, the fuller life is better; and she finds her duty in the endeavor to better the quality of life. She regards with sympathy, but not without criticism, the fierce physical desire that a race, a species, a family, shall inherit the earth, and sets herself apart as a disciple of the spirit to temper that animal heat with the cold impartiality of those who have no hope of animal immortality. By virtue of her isolation she is a critic. She denies that life fulfils its best function in procreation; she estimates life in itself, for itself; she judges each life as a whole complete in itself.

Take friendship with an old maid; it is not the

sunlight indeed, but there is in it a twilight calm, a cool, to be enjoyed, which a man can find in no other human relation. Parents are friends, but they cannot wholly shake off all shadow of constraint that comes from the respect and obedience due to their office : they are hedged about by the gap that must separate one generation from another. Children, likewise, are more and less than friends. Man for man has an affection, sometimes, like that of Montaigne for La Boétie of an intense and exalted character. But friendship for an old maid, in its comfortable freedom from the troubles of intemperate feeling, from the duties of a son, a husband, a father, a lover, gives the special charm and satisfaction derived from a different range of sensibilities, from the variety and interest of another series of thoughts and opinions. There is a singular sweetness in this contact with the unmating soul, in this pleasant introspect into the cool sequestered garden of a nunnery.

In conversation the old maid is not only unhampered by the immediate corollaries of maternity, diet, hygiene, and all the threads that weave the web and woof of home ; but she also may spread her wings in general freedom. She has no deep concern but her own soul, and may risk

the consequences of thought, of beliefs and dis-
beliefs, of imaginings and hopes. She enters
into a conversation for its own sake, accepting
it as an important matter for the time being committed to her charge. And her talk is steeped
with a fine flavor by her realization of human
relations; these are not taken for granted nor
neglected, neither magnified nor belittled, but
regarded as the principal business on our human
pilgrimage, as the materials out of which in the
main human lives are made.

Old maids are the best readers of books. A
mother reads a book, whether for knowledge, or
recreation, with the absent-mindedness of a shop-
per who holds a ribbon to the light, inwardly
pondering how its color will match the already pur-
chased stuff at home. An old maid has no such
preoccupations; for her a book stands on its own
feet, to be judged according to its service to her.
She reads biography, not for useful examples,
but for the human interest of a human life; history, not as the story of a world in which she is
but a steward of interests vested in the heir, but
of her own world; poetry, as an emanation from
the spirit of life, not merely as the blossoming
of the imagination in the mating season, that loses
its sweetness as soon as the married state has

become a matter of habit. In fact, all that books
deal with, like life itself, wears a different aspect
to the mother and to the old maid, for their morals
are of a different order : one has the morality of an
immortal humanity, the other that of the brief-
lived individual spirit, whose affair is not with the
future but the present. Manners come specially
within an old maid's care. They are the outward
manifestation of all human relations, and in most
of our relations with our fellows the outward manifestation is more important than the inward sentiment. Life consists in meetings with friends,
relations, acquaintances, strangers; and the one
art that can render these random meetings, the
chance crossings of our paths, anything but a
burden to hurrying travellers, we commit to no
special study or training, to no special group of
guardians and teachers. The old maid is the natural mistress of an *atelier* for manners. A mother's
manners are rubbed, scratched, and scarred by
affairs of far greater importance; the old maid's
manners have a lightness, a silvery sheen; and,
in her lack of preoccupation, she is able to understand their social use, she is free to study what
theories and methods may teach the rest of us
how to appreciate, at least how to recognize and
respect the art.

There is also the function of education. Watch the mother, see her at her board, cutting bread and pouring out tumblers of milk for half a dozen proofs of her loyalty to her theory; see her stitching, basting, darning, or computing next year's budget, with her mental eye fixed far on generations yet unborn. She, in obedience to her maternal instinct, not only feeds, clothes, and physics, but she also trains and teaches, drops into little open, twittering minds her own maternal theories; and even when her children grow into adolescence she wishes to guide and govern them according to her feelings. Her instinct may very well take care of them during the instinctive period of childhood, for children are likely to tread the great highroad of animal life; but for her to continue her control when they become reasoning beings is another matter. Instruction, the art of encouraging rational processes, of developing the character, of catching and fixing as a durable possession the winged idealism of youth, is a matter not for maternal zeal but for cool and sober impartiality. It is not in the school that this instruction is best given, but in the thousand opportunities that spring up in the companionship between the elder sister and the little brother, between the aunt and her nephew, between the old friend and the young; for in that companionship the boy's heart is unlocked, his affection leads his mind, and both heart and mind become docile and curious. The old maid, under the impulse of her celibate ideals, seeks to quicken the boy's individual soul, to teach him to regard dispassionately our social structure (built as it must be upon the animal conception of life), and above all to regard himself as a creature capable of individual completeness, whose essential problem in life is neither to procure for himself animal immortality nor to possess the earth, but to attain a conception of perfection.

This virginal attitude towards the instruction of children seems to illustrate the social usefulness of old maids, their general fitness to be critics of society. No one, of course, could suggest that they should be the only critics of social changes; that task would be out of all proportion to their numbers and to their powers, and not specially related to the trait that distinguishes them from other people. Their service is not to do the work of criticism, but to point out the right position for criticism to take, the right attitude to adopt. The unencumbered celibates more easily than others may climb the heights

of impartiality, from where by the dawning light
of justice, which as yet only lightens those
heights, they will command a full view of the social
situation as a whole. Take socialism, for instance; see wall upon wall, the ancient conceptions of caste and class and individualism, of
take-and-keep-that-can, deeply entrenched, honor-
ably and dishonorably fortified and defended,
which are built out of the dogma that children shall
succeed to parents in undiminished privileges and
prerogatives, and which rest on the foundation of
animal immortality; and see outside those walls the
men that have sons to inherit but no privileges to
bequeath. What greater need could there be for dispassionate guides detached from all loyalty to that
deep, fundamental passion of animal immortality?
In the social order, mothers, with their fierce maternal instincts and rich emotions, with their
disdain of reason, are constant supporters of passion on both sides; in great measure they determine the attitude and the action of men; so that,
if only to undo and counteract the influence of
their married sisters, old maids have much to do
here.

The difference between their hands is a fair
index to the differences between a mother and a
spinster in creed and deed, in friendship, educa-

tion, or critical usefulness. A mother's hand
with its tenderness, its caressing, smoothing, sooth-
ing, promises of warmth after cold, of comfort
after privation, of happiness after pain, with its
melodious rhythmic movement which lulls and
charms the troubled child, is the incomparable
instrument of the corporal sequence of life; her
hand strokes the child as if the whole service of
the precedent ages had been to shape and perfect it as an instrument of maternal love, as if the
great artist Time had bent over it, thought over it,
toiled over it, planned, modelled, devised, and
imagined, till with the ripeness of perfection, he
had rested content. The hand of the maid is
different. Its touch brings no corporeal promises,
its loneliness almost disturbs the animal within us,
and yet it seems fraught with something just beyond the power of touch to impart, as if touch
were struggling up into language, charged with a
message beyond our comprehension and a sympathy beyond our reach. Celibate fingers have
clasped no lover's hand, they have caressed no
child, they touch with the composure of the
evening wind, which nevertheless brings to us
the knowledge that it has touched great things
afar and will touch great things again, and in between touches us.

The touch of the old maid's hands, that once soothed and comforted our adolescent griefs and discontents, explains the deepest service which the celibate may render to society. She is free to devote herself to an ideal, to the ideal of the individual life, to a passionate renunciation of the corporal self and the passionate worship of *That*, which though we do not know it, or at least do not perceive it, yet may be. She has a priestly office to fill, not dissimilar to that of her elder sisters, the nuns, but more fructifying, more intelligent. It is the mission of her Celibate Order to go into the world to combat the original sin of our animal origin, which brings with it the greed, the grossness, the pride, the injustice, of animals that have prevailed in the struggle for existence. This Celibate Order is a modern priesthood, and our society, whatever its self-satisfaction and its self-confidence, is not wholly without the need of a priesthood. For the primary function of priesthood now, just as it has always been, is to maintain and encourage an acceptance of a belief in holiness. Priests, in theory at least, constitute a band set apart from the hurry and sweat of the ordinary day; they are hedged about by custom, seclusion, and reserve, in order that they shall publicly and privately, before men in con-

c

gregations, and among the chance companions of
daily life, teach by precept and example a belief
in holiness.

In former times, and even to-day by virtue of
inherited ideas, the priesthood has been confined
to men, but it has always derived its strength
from the support of celibate women. As Mary
and Martha to Jesus, as St. Scolastica to her
brother St. Benedict, as St. Clare to her brother
in the spirit, St. Francis, so women set apart from
the current of corporal life have always sustained
and comforted the priest. The more the course
of history sweeps the priesthood away from the
path of its old orbit, the greater the need that
ministering sisters shall perform the primary func-
tions of the priest in his stead. The dispassionate,
unprejudiced celibate must keep alive the belief
in the creed of holiness. Churches and dogmas
may go, but the conceptions embodied in the
sacraments remain. The entry into life is a
solemn and sacred matter: "La vie n'est ni un
plaisir ni une douleur, c'est une affaire grave dont
nous sommes chargés, qu'il faut conduire et termi-
ner avec honneur." If this is true — if life is
neither for pleasure nor pain, but an affair of consequence that we must carry on and end with
honor, who is so well-fitted as the old maid to teach

the child that his business in life is not worldly
success, nor popular applause, nor achievement
of obvious bulk, but to live his life as an affair of
honor. This is the creed of the old maid. She
asserts the dogma of personal spiritual responsibility, she proclaims the importance of the individual in himself, though the inheritance of
propulsion, of animal energy, which has descended
to him from time immemorial, perish with him
forever; she rejects the doctrine that humanity
as a whole is the only entity with a meaning, that
we are but constituent atoms, mere partakers in a
stream of physical life not our own, links in the
great procreative chain that binds the first life
on earth with the last. She is eminently the
priestess of spiritual life, and as such may render
the noblest services to humanity.

All such services proceed from the old maid's
idealism. By the renunciation of the greatest
human desire, of the greatest human happiness,
she has obtained spiritual freedom; she has not
misallied her soul, she has kept herself unspotted
from the world. This renunciation, which looks
to the vulgar ridiculous, to youth silly, to married
folks mistaken and melancholy, is no brief or easy
matter; it is a Purgatory, and the maiden soul
that passes through it becomes a gracious being.

DE SENECTUTE

Cato Major, *a man of fifty.*

Scipio
Lælius } *Students at Harvard College.*

Cato: Welcome, Scipio; your father and I were friends before you were born. And a hearty welcome to you, too, Lælius; all your family I esteem my kinsmen. Is this the holiday season, or how comes it that you have at this time shuffled off the coil of academic life?

Scipio: We have a few free days now according to the liberal usage of our college, and we have come, relying upon your kinship with Lælius, and your friendship for my father, to ask you some questions.

Cato: I had thought that seniors of Harvard College were more disposed to answer questions than to ask them; but I am truly glad that you have come, and as best I can, I will endeavor to satisfy your curiosity.

Lælius: We have been disputing, sir, in the interim between academic studies, as to the value of life; whether, taking it all in all, life should be regarded as a good thing or not. We are agreed that, so far as Youth is concerned, life is well worth the living, but we are doubtful whether, if Old Age be put into the same balance with Youth, the whole will outweigh the good of never having lived.

SCIPIO: You see that we have really come to ask you about Old Age, for as to Youth, that we know of ourselves.

CATO: About Old Age! Naturally that has been the subject of my meditations, and I will gladly impart my conclusions, such as they are.

SCIPIO: Thank you very much. I regret to say that we are obliged to take the next train back to town, so our time is all too short.

CATO: We have half an hour. I will waste no time in prologue. And I shall begin by asking Scipio's pardon, for I shall flatly contradict his assumption that the young have a knowledge of Youth.

SCIPIO: Of course we beg you to let neither our youth nor our opinions hamper the free expression of your views.

LÆLIUS: We are all attention, sir.

I

CATO: In the first place, my young friends, Age has one great pleasure which Youth (in spite

of its own rash assumption of knowledge) does
not have, and that is a true appreciation and
enjoyment of Youth.

You who are young know nothing of Youth.
You merely live it. You run, you jump, you
wrestle, you row, you play football, you use your
muscles, without any consciousness of the wonderful machinery set in motion. You do not perceive the beauty of Youth, the light in its eye, the
coming and going of color in its cheek, the ease
and grace of its movements. Nor do you appreciate the emotions of Youth. You are con-
tented or discontented, merry or sad, hopeful or
downcast; but whatever that *feeling* is, you are
wholly absorbed in it, you are not able to consider it objectively, nor to realize how marvelous
and interesting are the flood and ebb of youthful
passion.

In fact, the young despise Youth; they are
impatient to hurry on and join the ranks of that
more respectable and respected body, their immediate seniors. The toddling urchin wishes
that he were old enough to be the interesting
schoolboy across the way, who starts unwillingly
to school; the schoolboy, as he whistles on his
tedious path, wishes that he were a freshman, so
splendid in his knowledge, his independence, his

possessions, so familiar with strange oaths, so gloriously fragrant of tobacco. The freshman would be a sophomore. You seniors wish to be out in the great world, elbowing your way among your fellow men, busy with what seem to you the realities of life. Youth feels that it is always standing outside the door of a most delectable future.

Appreciation of Youth is part of the domain of art. There is no virtuoso like the old man who has learned to see the manifold beauties of Youth, the charm of motion, the grace of carriage, the glory of innocence, the fascination of passion. The world of art created by the hand of man has nothing that can challenge comparison with the masterpieces of Youth. No man, in his own boyhood, ever had as much pleasure from running across the lawn as he gets from seeing his sons run on that very spot; no laughter of his own was ever half so sweet to his ears as the laughter of his little girl. No man in his youth ever understood the significance of the saying, "Of such is the Kingdom of Heaven." You may smile condescendingly, young men, but in truth the appreciation of Youth is a privilege and possession of Old Age.

LÆLIUS: I did but smile in sympathy.

SCIPIO: If I understand you aright, Cato, Youth is a drama, in which the actors are all absorbed in their parts, while Age is the audience.

CATO: You conceive my meaning. The play is worthy for the gods to watch, — it out-Shaksperes Shakspere.

II

CATO: The second great acquisition that comes to Old Age is the mellowing and ripening of life.

As I look back across the years I can see that I and my friends were all what are called *individualists*. We were all absorbed in self, just as you young men are. We went through our romantic period in which self, with a feather in its cap and a red waistcoat, strutted over the stage. It monopolized the theatre; everybody else — parents, brothers, sisters, uncles, aunts, cousins, schoolmates — were supernumeraries, whose business was to look on while the hero recited his lines. With attention concentrated all on self, the youth is shy of all other youths, of everybody whose insolent egotism may wish to push its way upon his stage and interrupt his monologue. The *I* of Youth insists upon its exclusive right to emotion, upon its right to knowledge of the world at first-hand, upon its right to repeat the follies of its father, of its

father's father, of all its ancestors. Youth, bewildered by the excitement of self-consciousness,
can hardly see beyond the boundaries of self.

Youth is raw and suspicious. It looks askance
at its neighbors, is indifferent to their lot,
and delights in solitude, because solitude is
favorable to egotism. The young are ashamed
of their humanity. Boys regard the mass of boys
as if they were of a different species; they fight
shy of any general society among themselves;
they form cliques. The smallest clique is the
most honorable. And sacredly enshrined in the
very centre of the inner ring stands the Palla-
dium of self. You, Scipio, do not associate with
Gaius or Balbus, though they are the best scholars
in your class; nor do you, Lælius, frequent any
but the Claudii. From the vantage-ground, as
you think, of exclusiveness, you look down upon
your fellows herded in larger groups. You turn
up your aristocratic noses at the vulgarity of joy
in commonalty spread. Your judgments are
narrow, your prejudices broad; you are distrust-
ful and conservative; you are wayward and
crotchety; you are all for precedent, or all for
license. You rejoice in foolish divisions, your
country, your native province, your college, your
club, your way of doing things; you despise all

others, and all their ways. A boy represents the babyhood of the race; in him is incarnate the spirit of contempt for Barbarians.

Age is a reaction from the restive individualism of Youth. It recognizes the human inability to stand alone; it perceives that the individual is a bit broken from the human mass, that our ragged edges still maintain the pattern of the break, and are ready to fit into the general mass again. The old man no longer dwells on the differences between one human creature and his fellows; he reflects upon their common qualities. He finds no solace in isolation; he rejoices in community. Youth is supremely conscious of its own sensitiveness, its own palate, its own comfort, it is full of individual appetite and greed; but Age is conscious of humanity, of a universal sensitiveness, of palates untouched by delicacies, of bodies uncared for, of souls uncomforted, and its queasy stomach cannot bear to be helped tenfold, a hundredfold, a thousandfold, while fellow members of the indivisible body human sicken from want.

Age perceives a thousand bonds where Youth sees discord. Age sets store by the common good of life, it conceives of our common humanity as the mere right to share, and of pleasure as shar-

ing; it considers humanity partly as an enlarge-
ment of self, partly as a refuge from self; it
lightly passes over the differences of speech, of
accent, of clothes, of ways and customs, which to
boys like you, taken with the outward aspect of
the world, seem to erect such insuperable barriers
between them and their fellows. To Old Age
the sutures of humanity, that to the youthful
eye gape so wide, are all grown together, the
several parts are merged into one whole.

Of all pleasures, none is so satisfying as the
full enjoyment of our common humanity. It
loosens the swaddling clothes that wrap us round;
it alone gives us freedom. No doubt this is
partly due to the nearer approach of death; the
chill of night causes the pilgrim to draw nearer
his fellows and warm himself at the kindly
warmth of human fellowship. But be the cause
what it may, the enjoyment of humanity is a
taste that grows with man's growth; it is a part
of the ripening of life, and comes quickest to those
who ripen in the sun of happiness.

There is another element in this process of
mellowing with age. Old Age is intensely aware
of the delicacy of this human instrument, on
which fate can play all stops of joy and pain; it
feels an infinite concern before the vast sum of

human sentience; it sees in humanity the harvest of all the tillage of the past; it ponders over the long stretch of toil, cruelty, suffering, bewilderment, and terror, of unnumbered generations. All along its path life flickers up but to be quenched by death. In contemplation of this funeral march the old man nuzzles to the breast of humanity, and longs for more and more intimate human communion. To him humanity is not a mere collection of individual units, but a mighty organism, animated by a common consciousness, proceeding onward to some far-off end, with whose destiny his own is inseparably joined.

III

LÆLIUS: What do you say to the physical weakness of Old Age? Surely the lack of physical vigor is a disadvantage.

CATO: It is true, Lælius, that Old Age fences in a man's activities. We old men are no longer free to roam and amuse, or bore, ourselves with random interests. Our bounds are set. But with the diminishing of space comes what may well be a more than corresponding intensity of interest. The need of boundlessness is one of the illusions of youth; it is a consequence of youth's instability, of its unwillingness to hold its attention fixed. The tether of Old Age obliges us to fix our attention; and no matter on what our attention is set, we can find there concentrated the essential truths of the universe. The adjectives *great* and *small* are not God's words; they mark our inability to throw aside our egoism even for a moment.

The Japanese general who has slain his tens of thousands on the plains of Manchuria, squats on his hams and contemplates the infinite beauties in the iris, as the sunshine flatters it, or the breeze bellies out the wrinkled petals of its corolla. Its purple deepens, its white emulates the radiance of morning, its velvet texture outdoes the royal couch of fairyland, its pistil displays all the marvel of maternity, its laborious root performs its appointed task with the faithfulness of ministering angels. The armies of Russia and Japan could not tell as much concerning the history of the universe as does this solitary iris. A garden that will hold a lilac bush, a patch of mignonette, a dozen hollyhocks, or a few peonies, is enough to occupy a Diocletian. A square yard of vetch will reveal the most profound secrets of our destiny; the fermentation of a cup of wine discloses enough to make a man famous for centuries; the disease of a silkworm will determine the well-being of a kingdom; the denizens in a drop of blood cause half the sufferings of humanity. The achievements of modern science merely confirm the intuitions of Old Age. Littleness is as full of interest as bigness.

Youth has a longing for Sinai heights, for the virgin tops of the Himalayas, and the company of deep-breathing mountaineers; this is because he cannot see the wonder in common things. Blindly impatient with what he has, blindly discontented with what is about him, he postulates the beautiful, the real, the true, in the unattainable. But Old Age delights in what is near at hand, it sees that nothing is cut off from the poetry of the universe, that the littlest things throb with the same spirit that animates our hearts, that the word *common* is a mere subterfuge of ignorance.

LÆLIUS: If I conceive your meaning aright, Cato, Old Age is, through greater understanding, nearer the truth than Youth.

CATO: Yes, Age understands that such revelation as may be vouchsafed to man concerning the working of the will of the Gods needs not be sought on Olympus, but in whatever spot man is. Earth, the waters, the air, and all the starry space, are waiting to communicate the secrets of

the Gods to the understanding of man. Many
secrets they will reveal; and many, perhaps,
they will never disclose.

IV

SCIPIO: Excuse me, Cato, but are you not, in
substance, claiming the advantages of religion, and
is not religion as open to Youth as to Old Age?

CATO: By no means, Scipio; Old Age is
more religious than Youth. I do not speak of
the emotional crises that come upon young men
and young women in early youth; those crises
seem too closely related to physical growth and
development to be religious in the same sense in
which Old Age is religious. That the emotional
crises of Youth may bear as truthful witness to
the realities of the universe as the temperate
religion of Old Age, I do not deny. The God
that Youth sees by the light of its emotional fires
may be the real God, but that image of God is
transitory, it appears in fire and too often dis-
appears in smoke. The image of God that appears to Old Age is a more abiding image; it
reveals itself to experience and to reason instead
of to the sudden and brief conviction of vision.
Old Age finds God more in its own image, calm,
infinitely patient, not revealed merely by the

vibrant intensity of passion, but in the familiar and the commonplace. To Old Age the common things of life declare the glory of God.

Common things affect different minds differently; yet to most minds certain familiar phenomena stand out conspicuous as matter for reflection. Most extraordinary of all common things is human love. Throughout the universe of the stellar sky and the universe of the infinitely little, so far as we can see, there is perpetual movement, change, readjustment; and, except for our animal life, the whole machinery whirls along without a throb of emotion, without a touch of affection. Why should not men have been mechanical, swept into being and borne onward, by the same energies, in the same iron-bound way? Even if consciousness, unfolding out of the potential chaos that preceded man, was able to wheedle an existence from Necessity, why was it expedient to add love? Would not mechanical means serve the determined ends of human life, and impel us to this action and to that, without the need of human affection? Human affection is surely a very curious and interesting device.

And if the world must be peopled, and the brute law of propagation be adopted in a universe of chemistry and physics, why was it neces-

sary to cover it with visions of " love and of honor
that cannot die," and to render the common man
for the moment worthy of an infinite destiny?

Then there is also the perplexity of beauty.
Why to creatures whose every footstep is determined by the propulsions of the past, should a
flower, a tuft of grass, a passing cloud, a bare tree
that lifts the tracery of its branches against a sun-
set sky, cause such delight? Descended from an
ancestry that needed no lure of beautiful sight
or of pleasant sound to induce it to live its appointed life, why should mankind become so
capriciously sensitive?

Or consider human happiness. Here, for example, I live, in this little cottage that seems to
have alighted, like a bird, on the slope of this
gentle hill. Red and white peonies grow before
the door, enriching the air with their fragrance.
They charm both me and the bees. In yonder
bush beside the door a chipping-sparrow sits
upon her nest; and in the swinging branch of the
elm tree overhead two orioles rear their brood,
and as they flash by, their golden colors delight
the human beings that watch them. Look over
that stone wall, and mark how its flat line gives
an incomparable effect to the landscape. See our
New England fields dotted with New England

D

elms; and far beyond see those white-sailed
schooners scud before the boisterous wind. The
farmer's boy, who fetches milk and eggs, left me
that nosegay of wild flowers. Look! Look!
See how the whiteness of that cloud glorifies
the blue of the sky. Is it not strange that
all these things, that go about their own business, should, by the way, perform a work of
supererogation and give us so much unnecessary
pleasure?

The young do not see or do not heed these common things; they are busy with their own emotions.
Youth is a time of tyrannical demands upon the
universe. It expects a perpetual banquet of
happiness, and at the first disillusion charges the
universe with falsehood and ingratitude. It no
sooner discovers that all creation is not hurrying
to gratify its impulses, than it cries out that all
creation is a hideous thing. It arraigns the universe; it draws up an indictment of countless
crimes. The long past becomes one bloody
tragedy. Dragons of the prime rend one another, creature preys upon creature, all things
live at the expense of others, and death is the
one reality. All the records of the earth tell a
tale of bloody, bestial cruelty. The globe is
growing cold; man shall perish utterly, all his

high hopes, all his good deeds, all his prayers,
all his love, shall become as if they had never
been. And Youth, because the universe for a
moment seems to neglect it, in a Promethean
ecstasy defies the powers that be.

But Old Age, rendered wiser by the mellowing years, concerns itself less with the records of
palæontology and the uttermost parts of the universe, than with matters at closer range and
more within its comprehension. It fixes its eye
less on death than on life. It considers the phenomena of love, of beauty, of happiness, and the
factors that have wrought them, and its thoughts
trace back the long, long sequence of causes that
lie behind each contributing factor; they follow
them back through recorded time, back through
the ages of primitive man, through the dim
times of the first stirrings of organic life, through
vast geological periods, back to chaos and old
night. They follow each contributory factor out
through the universe, to the uttermost reaches
of space, beyond the boundaries of perception;
and everywhere they find those contributory
causes steadily proceeding on their several ways
through the vast stretches of space and time, and
combining with other factors from other dark
recesses of the unknown, in order, at last, to pro-

duce love, beauty, happiness, for such as you
and me. Consider, you young men, who pass
these miracles by as lightly as you breathe, this
marvellous privilege of life, the infinite toil and
patience that has made it what it is, and then, if
you dare, call the power that animates the universe cruel.

V

SCIPIO: I perceive, Cato, that you believe in a
God, a God in sympathy with man, and I grant
— Lælius, too, will grant — that such a belief, if
a characteristic of Old Age, does indeed give Old
Age one great advantage over Youth.

CATO: No, I cannot claim that a belief in God
is a necessary accompaniment of Old Age, but I
think that Old Age is far more likely than Youth
to dwell upon the considerations that fit in with
such a belief.

To Youth all the energy of the universe is in-
explicable, the things we behold are the products
of blind forces; but to Old Age the essential element in the universe is the potential character of
its infinitely little constituent parts. Out of the
dust came the human eye, up from the happy
combination of the nervous system came the
human mind, and with the passage of time has
come the new organic whole, humanity. Do not

these phenomena hint at a divine element in the
potential energies of the universe? What is all
this motion and turmoil, all the ceaseless turn-
ings and tossings of creation, but restless discontent and an endeavor to produce a higher
order? Our human love, beauty, and happiness
are less to be explained by what has gone before
than by what is to come. You cannot explain the
first streaks of dawn by the darkness of the night.
All the processes of change — gases, vapors,
germs, human souls — are the perturbations of
aspiration. This vibrant universe is struggling
in the throes of birth. As out of the dust has
come the human soul, so out of the universe shall
come a divine soul. God is to be the last fruits
of creation. Out of chaos He is evolving.

You would laugh at me, Scipio, if it were not
for your good manners. Wait and learn. Belief
in deity is, in a measure, the privilege of us old
men. Age has lost the physical powers of Youth,
and no one will dispute that the loss is great, but
that loss predisposes men to the acceptance of
religious beliefs. Physical powers, of themselves,
imply an excessive belief in the physical universe;
muscles and nerves, in contact with unyielding
things, exaggerate the importance of the physical
world. Throughout the period of physical vigor

the material world is a matter of prime consequence; but to an old man the physical world
loses its tyrannical authority. The world of
thought and the world of affection rise up and
surpass in interest the physical world. In these
worlds the presence of God is more clearly dis-
cernible than in the material world; but if He
is in them, He will surely come into the material
world.

Even now, here and there, His glory is visible.
A mother, at least, cannot believe that the throbs
of her heart over her sick child are of no greater
significance than the dropping of water or the
formation of a crystal. The presence of deity
has reached her heart; in course of time, it will
also reach the water and the crystal. If matter
of itself has produced the passion of human love,
it surely may be said, without presumption, to be
charged with potential divinity.

Old Age cares less and less for the physical
world; it lives more and more in the worlds of
thought and of affection. It does not envy
Youth, that lives so bound and confined by
things physical. But you have been very patient.
Make my compliments to your families, and perhaps in part to Harvard College, on your good
manners, and remember when you, too, shall be

old, to have the same gentle patience with Youth
that you now have with Old Age.

SCIPIO: Thank you, Cato.   If we are not con-
vinced, we desire to be.

LÆLIUS: Yes, indeed, we now doubt that those
whom the Gods love die young.

CATO: You must hurry or you will miss your
train.   Good-bye.

THE RELIGION OF THE PAST

I

THE religion of the future is occupying men's minds. They are right to think of it, to talk of it, and hope for it; their leaders, as leaders toward the new have always been, are men of the pioneer sort, animated by a need of room, eager to avoid and escape from the restraining bounds, the narrow quarters, in which the old centuries have lodged us. They are brave; they set their faces toward the new, and feel the fresh salt breezes of the unknown sea blow full in front. Their courage is none the less praiseworthy because at times it seems to shine the more from contrast with the dull hues of a sicklier liver; nor is their self-reliance less to be admired because it is quickened by a knowledge of the self-helplessness of others. They are leaders; their business is to lead, and one of their duties is to prod the laggards and the stay-at-homes. They have so much right upon their side, that they may well be excused for thinking they have it all.

The need of change, of cutting away old, time-
eaten parts of religion, of replacing that which is
cut away by modern notions, of substituting
dogmas that will stand the hammers of logic and
science for those that dissolve impalpable before
a child's knowledge of physics and history, is and
may well be ample justification for a wide sweep
of the pioneer axe. They, however, by the very
thoroughness of their devastation, force the issue
of the value of this thoroughness. Their trenchant
ploughshares uncover our holes and crevices,
and stir the dispossessed "wee, sleekit, cowrin',
tim'rous" acceptors of old ideas into an attitude
of asking for further proof of this light-hearted
confidence in the new. Is there not some small
remnant of religious use left in the old home?
Have the emigrants got it all stowed away in their
lockers?

For if, by this uncompromising thoroughness,
they raise a comparison between themselves
and us, if they vaunt their riches in contrast
to our poverty, they must be scrupulous to
measure, and set apart, the things that are
theirs on one side and the things that are ours
on the other. There must be no confusion.
The produce of the new land whither they go
is theirs; the produce of the old home and its

garden belongs to us. Let us divide clearly and mark the division.

The new religion has a "god"; but at the very outset we may ask, What right have they to take our name? How can they strip that name of a hundred associations that come thronging, — the belief of good men, the hopes of the unhappy, the trust of the valiant, the passion of those who set their hearts upon the things that are not of this world? What is their "god"? They feel the pulse and throb of countless forces, they feel their sensibilities played upon, their consciousness awake and receptive, their fires of life fed with fuel; they assert that all these unknown commotions, these stirrings, waves, fluctuations, movements, are the results of contact with innumerable manifestations of one primal force, and they say he is their god. But this very zeal for unification, for oneness, for an all-embracing whole, is of our creation; we of the past have created that. They of the future have only a vast aggregate of like elements, if even they have that. They combine and mould together in one form these inorganic, intolerant forces, and then they wrap this moulded image up in our emotions, in the reverence and awe that we of the old home have made. Reverence, awe, love, are the mak-

ings of the past, the handiwork of ignorance, of
superstition, of belief, of faith; they are ours to
deck our altars and our idols.

The "god" of the future is but a concatenated
aggregate of unknown forces, and both aggrega-
tion and concatenation are assumptions. They
claim reverence for the reign of law, with its uniform and measured impartiality, in place of the
arbitrary and tyrannical actions of a jealous God;
but they have no right to reverence. Even if
they will kneel to the downward fall of an apple,
and the elliptical orbits of the planets, even if they
will sing hymns to the swell and ebb of the tide,
and praise the union of hydrogen and oxygen, they
have no right to take our words, our associations,
our frippery of old thoughts and emotions. Unless they are prepared to bestow an adequate
allotment of ecstasy on each electric volt, they
have no right to clap all the volts together in one
symbolic whole and bow down before them. The
only rational attitude toward the "god" of the
future is distrust. That god must be utterly
dehumanized and given its due, no more, no less.
"It" should inspire such amazement and respect
as generalizations of the human mind, made in the
laboratory or the lecture-room, are entitled to.
"It" must be charged with whatever sin and

suffering, whatever pain and distress, there may
be throughout the universe. "It" may well be
feared by the timid and should be defied by the
bold. "It" cannot attach to itself any of the
emotions that the religion of the past has called
into being. We are men, and the relation of humanity toward the universal forces is one of
enmity. We must conquer or die. We must
outwit them, control them, counteract them, or
they will beat us down under their feet. There
is no evidence of any friendliness toward us; those
forces, for which the reign of law is emotionally
claimed, will destroy us according to their laws
unless we can control them. We are human, they
are non-human; this is all we know.

In this respect the reformers have taken from
our stock what belongs to us; but by their own
doctrine they may not take a word, — the word
of words, — transfer it to their stock, and then
pretend that they have taken a mere term of
dialectics, as if they could leave behind the con-
notation which is its essence, and strip off all
vestiges of those yearnings which *semper, ubique
et ab omnibus* have given the word god all its
significance. Then on this borrowed word they
seek to build the religion of the future.

What attribute of religion can they hang upon

it, they who have cut themselves loose from all the
network of affection that man's history has
woven about the God of the past? They cannot
take duty. Their god has nothing in common
with duty; the two conceptions are antagonistic.
Their god acts on motives that we can neither
know nor conjecture; this present manifestation
of contemporaneous phenomena that we call our
universe comes from we know not where, and goes
we know not whither. All is dark. But duty is
plain and readily understood. Duty is a human
conception, a means for human good, a human
contrivance in the long war of humanity against
the forces of evil that encompass us on every side.
Good is that which is good to humanity; evil is
that which is evil to it. The unconscious forces
that nourish germs of disease, that rob us of health,
of happiness, of life, that cause untoward heat and
cruel cold, that "hurl the lightnings and that wing
the storms," that create venomous reptiles and
poison-bearing insects, that cool the old earth and
threaten our race with a miserable end, are to our
human desires wholly evil. They are all law-
abiding, and in them as well as in us lies a portion
of the dignity of the universe; and yet we hate
them. Our duties are toward our parents and
children, toward our wives and husbands, toward

our fellow townsfolk, toward such as chance may render our neighbors, toward our horses and our dogs. Out of earthly relations our duties are begotten; but out of what shall we create a notion of duty toward this "god," or how shall we, except by making ourselves mere fate-led puppets, identify duty with its will? Our human duties, our sense of solidarity, our consciousness of common joys and sorrows, are not affirmations of this new "god," but a denial of it. If we shall awake, as the reformers say we shall, to a keener appreciation of the need of standing by one another, of working together, it will be because we perceive that we are alone, unaided, sailing in one great ship over an unknown sea. The sense of human duty may grow stronger as we shall cease to rely on outside help, we may become more self-reliant under the new gospel; but self-reliance is not religion.

II

The religion of the past is of a different order. It was born of ignorance and superstition, nursed by credulity and need, fostered and tended by evil times, by misery, disappointment, fear, and death. Nothing could be further from a rational and scientific explanation of this extraordinary phenomenon, life, than the God of old. He grew with

the growth of our race, he acquired attributes as
we progressed, he gradually became high, holy,
and loving; and, when, in our deeper need to
feel communion with Him, He put on human shape
and shared our common human experiences, man
loved Him passionately. He is the creation of
many great hearts; and because humanity has
made Him, we love Him. Humanity has loved
its beautiful creation; and, rounding out the
allegory, created a human mother for its offspring.
We feel our weakness, our ignorance, our incapac-
ity to stand alone, and we cling to that which we
have created.

   Yet because we can see no further than our own
handiwork, because we seem to have been creating
something out of nothing, is it necessarily so?
And if it is so, was the handiwork a waste of labor
and of love?   Is the image of a loving God with a
human heart, botched and marred though it is by
the glosses of churchmen, necessarily an unservice-
able illusion?   How are we to know that it is an
illusion? What is this world? What are illusions, what is the line that divides them from other
impressions, and are not illusions as worth while
as other things?   Are they not oddly like reality,
and have they not their special uses? What is
our conscious life, but a storehouse of illusions,

and what are our senses but mechanical doors to let more illusions in ? Why should we not, for our comfort, our well-being, our ennoblement, create one illusion the more ?

Or ought not our old religion to be called a work of art rather than a cluster of illusions ? Is it not the incomparable work of the imagination, upon which, as upon speech, all men have been at work ? Here and there, indeed, great men have altered the design, remodelling sometimes the fundamental plan; while all the time, here and there, according to their personal tastes and capacities, the mass of believers have been adding touches: filling in the background, heightening the color, strengthening a line, or deepening a shadow. Is not this work of art a beautiful thing in itself, with all its rudeness and crudity ; and is it not so entwined and entangled with the history of the human race that any divorce between them must be a maim ?

They may prove without any great fear of opposition that the tribal god was a barbarous conception, that a national god is at times an irrational and mischievous hinderance to the progress of civilization. But why not proceed, as nature does, from seed to shoot, from shoot to stalk, from stalk to trunk, drinking in from sunshine and rain new

properties and powers, till the climber climbing
to its topmost bough sees ever further and further?
If we have grown, the tribal god has aided our
growth. In the home, in the school, in the
counting-room, in the court-house, on the battle-
field, or in the penitential cell, he or his successors
have helped men and women, boys and girls,
to fight the good fight. When Israel conquered
Moab, when Greece defeated Persia, when confederate Europe beat back the Huns, when a
high-aspiring soul has turned away from temptation, were not these victories touched at least with
the glory of divine achievement? It is important
for the right to prevail, even if in the doubtful
balance the right leans to one side only by the
least fraction of a scruple. Whenever the side
impregnated with a greater degree of high purpose
and aspiring will has overcome the other, that has
been a victory for the divine cause. Whenever
a man has sacrificed himself or what he loved most,
in obedience to the command of what he held
holy, whenever he has renounced the easy pleasure
for the hard denial, whenever the little persistent instincts of sympathy and human fellowship have triumphed over his passions, there the
tribal god, the national god, the sectararian god,
or the human god, has been by his side, helping

E

sustaining, encouraging. Wherever men have felt
that the issues before them were fraught with
a significance greater than the balance and adjust-
ment of appetite and expedience, there one of the
old gods was at work. The God of the past was
human. He cared for men, their tears, their endeavors, their love, their obedience; but the god of
the future is to have no human sympathies. From
now on, man is not to rely on God but on himself,
and we are now to watch the deceitful vapors,
that have set themselves together in the shape of
walls, bastions, ramparts, and bannered citadel,
dissolve in the white light of disillusion. The
real and the non-real must be set sharply apart.

The old religion had a mass of additions, accre-
tions, agglutinations, gathered to it as it rolled
along the path of history. These were unjustifi-
able in any logical system of theology; but why
should we adopt a manner of judgment that judges
according to origins? Why should we not judge
according to results? That has been an old habit
of mankind. When men felt a relief, an enlarge-
ment, a revival, a more potent energy, a new and
kindling vigor, they ascribed these accessions of
life to an animating power of goodness, and fell
upon their knees and worshipped it. They
invented the word *sacred* to define, as well as a

single word might do, these animating influences;
and when, after an habitual association of the felt
effects and the imagined causes, they desired to
experience again the remembered blessings, they
invoked the symbol of these causal circumstances
and hastened on the consequence. They established ceremonies in the hope of putting themselves
and their children in the way of receiving the
benignant gifts of the Spirit. They kept old
traditions, usages, terms, and practices, as a
grown man calls his father and his mother "papa"
and "mamma"; and by unreasonable association
of sentiments they swelled childish emotions into
manly deeds. It may even be that these superstitious imaginings of the past were instinctive
recognitions of forces uncomprehended, happy
reachings out for spiritual sustenance, and erron-
eous only in the explanation of their nature;
that they really found a way to draw upon secret
sources of power and life.

What is less reasonable than baptism? But if
a man has been baptized, and his father, and his
father's father, and his again, then the memory
of these repeated dedications of young life, — the
memory of young and radiant mothers praying
and smiling as they prayed, — from a time back
beyond all records, renders the ceremony more

potent in its effect upon the imagination than any argument drawn from common sense. Such ceremonies do not square with reason; they quicken deep emotions and bring their rude barbarian strength to the support of right doing. Men who stroll across the fields of Gettysburg and mark the contours of the hills, the slope of the falling ground, and feel their feet press the very sods pressed by the dead and dying on those three great days, do not ask whether on that summit a factory might be built, on this meadow grain planted, and along that ancient line of fence a highway laid out; they stop, and highly resolve to quit themselves like men on whatever field the battle of life may chance to range them.

If men are moved to adhere to the cause of right because of visions and dreams of other men who died long ago, if they are cheered and emboldened because they wear a uniform, follow a flag, and tramp to the rolling of sticks beaten on taut pigskin, why not keep these beneficial supports, irrational though they are? A thousand chances every day remind us that we are not creatures of reason, but act willy-nilly in response to innumerable stimuli that prick us from we know not where.

Marriage under the new dispensation will not be a sacrament. But is not this a question of words? How is a man, in the full flood of romantic passion, going to formulate with any pretense of fitness the sentiments that draw him high above the meannesses of life, unless he calls on God to witness, and vows to love, honor, and cherish, forever? These rites are stammering efforts to give expression to sentiment. Never again is God revealed so present to man and woman, never again is a moment in their wedded lives so sacred. No man knows a sentiment except at the moment when he feels it; the most vivid imagination falls hopelessly short of another man's passion or even of his own remembered emotions. If passion is to be expressed in form or word, it must be by him whom the passion at the moment possesses; and to him love is of God and eternal.

In the new religion there are to be no intermediaries between God and man, none to whom, by self-dedication and long ministration, the habits of self-sacrifice, of aspiration, of willing unworldly things, of obeying high impulses, shall have become a power and an authority fit to help those whom the common occupations of life encumber; none to whom music, poetry, gratitude, and love

are daily cares, to whom the old trappings of
holiness are especially dear. God will be so
immanent in nitrogen and carbon, in drop of
water and puff of smoke, that nothing else will be
necessary; we need no intermediary to feel heat
or cold, to catch waves of light and sound, and
such other vibrations as do not elude us. The
alderman will register the names of our children,
the mayor our contracts for the reproduction of our
kind, the sheriff's deputy may superintend the
cremation of our bodies. Churches, purged from
superstition, fetiches, and idolatry, will be turned
into parlors for summer lectures, as in the golden
age swords were beaten into ploughshares; and
chapels will become reading-rooms with scientific
tracts on the tables and the best literature on the
shelves. Surgeons, physicians, dentists, and other
health officers of society, will satisfy the rational
needs of mankind; and the ignorant yearnings,
the unintelligible appetites, that have cried aloud
for a draught that shall satisfy them, will atrophy
for lack of pampering.

III

Above all, in this new religion there shall be
no mystery. Along the periphery of this luminous
spot, which our senses shine upon, we shall, to be

sure, still continue to come into direct contact
with the dark and the unknown; but we shall let
it alone. Like well-behaved children, we shall
not concern ourselves with what is not set on the
table before us. The old, foolish, passionate cry
demanding to know why, why, why, do I suffer
pain? Why am I called out of the tranquil insen-
tient mass into this sentient being, merely to feel
my nerves quiver and shrivel in the fires of grief,
disappointment, sorrow, jealousy, and shame?
Why, oh, why, am I? And what art Thou, dread
power by whose will I live? These futile questions, obviously asked far too often, will be
dropped. In fact, mystery is to be ignored.
Men, who in love and longing fling themselves
away from the things they know on the bosom
of mystery, stretching their arms toward the great
dark, are no longer to be tolerated. All the cor-
relatives of mystery — awe, reverence, holiness
— must depart together with mystery. And yet
what is knowledge, what at any moment and how
large is the content of consciousness? Are we
to live, incurious islanders, forever satisfied to turn
our faces inland and forswear the long encircling
beach, where the waves of mystery forever beat
and ocean winds bend the fringing trees, shaking
their tops to sibylline utterance?

And is our reasoning self the most intimate part of us, the most permanent and central? Is that the axis of our revolving life, to which moment by moment new sensations are fastened, and from which memories are sloughed off? Is that the tube through which the wind of life passes, catching its melody from chance stops by the way? Why then does the call of a bird, or the note of a violin, stir us so profoundly? There is a pleasure in the dark, a joy in the night, a relief from the inadequacy of waking, a freedom from the thraldom of sight and speculation. It is only through mystery and in mystery that man has the feeling of buoyancy, of an all-embracing being that bears him up, of an imagined contact with something unfathomable. In the light of day, staring at the outward aspects of such things as are within his horizon, he feels the littleness of his possessions, of his interests, of himself and his universe, he feels their insipidity and futility.

All the phenomena that astronomy, physics, chemistry, open their windows on derive their qualities from man. The stars and the interstellar spaces are glorious and awe-inspiring, because man is here to feel the glory and the awe. The minutest elements that reveal themselves to the chemist are marvellous because of our ignorance.

This universe, unreflected in any intelligence, moving unknown, unthinking, and unthought, would be an immeasurable *ennui*. It is the human relation that flatters the mountain-tops of science and gilds its discoveries with heavenly alchemy. The marvellous is merely our first acquaintance with the unfamiliar. But mystery is out of the category of the marvellous. Man, in face of that which transcends his intelligence, experiences a rest from effort, a peace; he feels the impotence of vexation and of striving. A pervasive calm that cannot be shaken wraps him round; he is free from the importunity of his senses. Neither sight, nor sound, nor movement, nor dimension, nor scope for activity, disturbs him; nothing is present but a fading consciousness that self seems slowly drifting from him. As when a long-drawn note upon a violin is held until the hearer no longer hears whether it continues or has ceased, and this uncertainty fills his attention; so man, confronting the mystery that encompasses all existence, absorbed and self-forgetful, insensibly doubts whether it and he are or are not. As the mind is refreshed and inspired by sleep, by exile from things and images, by submersion in self-unconsciousness, so, too, in the presence of mystery, loosed from the oppression of the familiar and the known, lifted above the friction and the fret of petty cause and consequence, the mind, grasping nothing, touching nothing, feeling but freedom, is refreshed and inspirited.

From this bath of his soul, man comes back to earth and daily life purified and ennobled. The trivial has a glint of some far-off meaning, the common loses the texture of its commonness, and our animal life — the needs and appetites of the body — becomes the symbol of something that shall justify toil and sacrifice. It is for this that creeds have gone beyond the verge of common-sense and practical understanding in their endeavors to find some symbol to express the incomprehensible. And if you once grant the significance of mystery, — that it transcends experience and cannot be classed in this order of phenomena or in that, — then why not let each man adjust his relations with it as he thinks or feels to be the best for him? Let him express his approach, his envisagement, his reactions, all his relations with mystery, in such forms and ways as he pleases; let him take such aids to further what to him is a desirable state of being as his experience shall counsel. There is still, for some people at least, in the vaulted nave, in the exultant, heavenward leap of the pointed arches, in the glory of color, in the long, deep rolling of the organ, a power that awakens dormant capacities for worship. Even in the little wayside church, where friends have met together for years, where the last words have been said over the well-beloved dead, where vows have been plighted, where babies have cooed at the minister while the young parents gazed proudly at each other, there is a touch of poetry that pushes back some bolt in the heart and opens the door to higher purposes. "Open wide the door of my heart that Thou mayst enter in," said St. Augustine. What matter, so long as the door is opened, whether it is music, liturgy, ritual, the blending sweetness of sad and happy memories, or some rational key, that opens the door?

Another distinction between the old religion and the new is the attitude toward pain. Under the old, often, oddly enough it is true, pain was regarded as the gift of God, something to be accepted with humility and resignation. Death, disease, disappointment were, if not marks of special favor, marks of special interest. Under the new religion, pain is a base inconvenience, an ignoble discomfort, to be removed speedily and completely. Nobody will quarrel with the attempt to remove pain as speedily and as

completely as possible.   Pain hinders living and
loving, and is an evil.   But we have not yet
succeeded in removing pain, and there is no
prospect that we shall.   Death, disease, discontent, coolness betwixt lovers, the indifference of
friends, the broken promises of life, are not to be
got rid of.   How had we best look upon such pains
while we endure them ?   Shall we regard them as
a tear in a garment, a leak in a pipe, as a mere base
inconvenience, or may we do as the old religion
teaches, and try to climb up on them as steps to a
fuller and larger life ?   The place of pain in natural
philosophy, whether it be a link in the chain of
human action or a mere register to record a backward step, is not of great consequence to us.   If
from pain we can call forth resolutions that free
us from the bonds of lust, of gluttony, or other
bestiality, if we can use it as a background from
which the colors of life stand out in greater charm,
or as the death of old life from which newer and
better life springs up, why should we not let the
gains shine back upon that liberating and fertiliz-
ing pain, and dignify it with the name of blessing ?
Why not deem it good in its own bitter way as the
Christians do, and let gratitude cluster about it,
and praise it as a condition and a help to the birth
of higher life ?

To reject this old use of pain because it is superstitious in origin, to refuse to make it our servant because we cannot banish it, is wasteful, and, being wasteful, blameworthy. Does not the desirable future, the happy land beyond the horizon of the present, show more clearly to the spirit in pain ? Does this not see — purified from the distractions, the temptations, the misconceptions that dog the steps of happiness and content — what is right, what is just, what is good ? To strike from human history the records of pain, the refinement, the ennoblement of man by suffering, when that has been accepted as a means of grace, would cheapen that history indeed. Self-sacrifice, too, must go. Its remote prototype, human sacrifice, its closer analogies, the holocaust of beeves, the blood of goats, the burning of incense, are common arguments to show us how superstitious the practice is.

The new theology is surely right in this : We must either reject or accept the principle of sacrifice. If we reject the principle, we commit ourselves to the doctrine of the right of each to the fullest enjoyment of life that he can attain. No man is to make way for anything less strong than himself, or to sacrifice himself, or anything that is his, for another's good. If we accept the principle, we can ill justify our course by reason. For we cannot consistently stop at arbitrary limits to sacrifice, as for the good of a higher being, of the community, of society at large, saying that so far sacrifice is good but no further.   And if we carry it out to logical completeness we also run foul of reason; for it is contrary to reason to sacrifice every member of a society for the sake of all; and it is still more absurd for each generation to sacrifice itself for the sake of the next; for then the long results of sacrifice would accumulate for the ultimate descendants of the human race, until the last man should finally experience the last satisfaction in solitude.

We can justify sacrifice only on the principle that there is in sacrifice some element of good for the sacrificial victim, some breath of a larger life, some draught of a nobler existence, some light from a higher sphere, if only for a time, how short soever.   Society may, indeed, punish its members who refuse to sacrifice themselves for the common weal so sternly that they shall be afraid to disobey; but then the doctrine of self-sacrifice will be destroyed.   Or, society may inculcate by education a willingness to die or suffer for the general good, but that is by an appeal to superstition and bigotry of an order wholly analogous to those religious superstitions which the new theology rejects. Unless we become pure egotists, we are forced to come very close to the Christians; for what reason is there for preferring altruism to egotism other than the witness of experience that to common men altruism offers a deeper and more intense emotional life?

Under the old religion, sacrifice was not judged by its origin. It was regarded as justifying itself. For, if what was sacrificed was a mere passing pleasure, a desire, an ambition, then, the appetite once passed, the sacrifice left barely a ripple on the memory, and the sense of self-mastery, of an easy wheel that lightly turns the ship, amply repaid the loss. If the sacrifice was serious, even to death, it was an oblation to duty and to the God from whom duty emanated. Sacrifice was not a loss; it was at most a displacement, a changing about, a shift; it added a more than compensating increase of power to some other member of the mystic body of which the willing victim was a part. He served his God, and his God blessed him. When the soul labors under an overwhelming emotion, words are idle and music is weak, and there is no voice to express the joy and rapture of love and worship, except sacrifice. It sounds unreasonable, but if we delve deep into human nature, we find strange correlations, odd fellowships of experience and sentiment.

This fresh rejection of the notions of sacrifice, of holiness, of mystery, of sacraments, of a divine presence, of the spiritual uses of pain, is a recurrence of the familiar attempt to put human life on one plane, to reduce it to one scale of values, to render it intelligible, subject to demonstration, to a final philosophy. It is the working of the positive mind, which is impatient of the sceptical and the undecided, and, out of desire to have things settled, inclines to any law rather than to anarchy, to any order rather than chaos, to any scheme of reason rather than to superstition. It proceeds from a bent for action; it must be up and doing, it must have a course, it must hoist sail and away, with chart, compass, and pole-star. But the sea-captain, however great his experience, however wide his knowledge, is obliged to stay upon the watery floor between the sea beneath and the air above. He is out of his element when he transfers his reckonings to religion. There are so many sides to life, so many sorts of experience, so many kinds of character, disposition, and temperament, so many different conceptions of what constitutes happiness and the value of life, that one might well leave the slow adjusting mind to continue to piece and patch the old constitution of his belief, changing it here and there, mending and tinkering, but preserving the main fabric which for centuries has procured him peace or victory and honor. Old conditions, the easy, rambling, comfortable habitation of the human heart, overgrown with memories and affections, if pulled down to make way for a modern structure, would leave desolation and barrenness. The lares and penates would not come to the new hearth.

IV

This discord between the old religion and the new is really, in one aspect at least, a reappearance of the contention over fact and poetry. To some men poetry is idle, deceitful, tending to senti- mental mooning, a hinderance to doing, a barrier to achievement, and beneficent only in its sterner aspects, as filling the soul with Miltonic images and a high disdain; to other men poetry — the poetry of childhood, of romance, of daring and delicacy, of far-off scenes and idolized images, of unattainable visions and momentary dreams, of lights and shadows that never were on land or sea, of hopeless causes and impossible beliefs — seems the best justification of life; and the old religion

F

is poetry. And poetry is a word of far-reaching meaning. The poet is a man upon whom the throbs of human experience beat with a clearer and more melodious resonance than upon other men. His imagination, led by a happy craving for harmony between these resonant experiences, selects and arranges, creating a melody; then, proceeding from melody to melody, he constructs a synthesis of sweet, concordant strains, and to these, as the echoes swell through his brain, an ideal significance attaches. The flush of color when dawn kisses the earliest clouds, the wave of sound when the breeze stirs the ripples and bends the rushes, the sensation of touch when hand meets hand, do not and cannot of themselves satisfy the yearnings they awaken; echoes, circling and rising, proceed onward and upward — till the memory of each, almost divorced from its origin, becomes to the exultant imagination a message from the infinite.

This ideal metempsychosis comes over all the great experiences of life; ideas, thus begotten, like some divine pollen, leaven as they permeate, and give a new aspect to common joys and pains, to right and wrong, to love and duty. Emotion, skilful musician, touches notes which in themselves are idle, until the hearer is banished from

the world of bald experience into an ideal world of
transcendent values. This ideal world becomes
more important, more real than the phenomena of
daily experience, lightly undergone and lightly
forgotten. It is the dreamer's dominant habitation, it becomes his home; and by it he explains
the trivial sequences of physical sensations.
Because in this ideal universe there is a God,
because there is an immortal life, because right is
right forever, and wrong, wrong, therefore human
life, the relations of man to man, the satisfactions
and discomforts of conscience, the success or
failure of the soul, are matters of mighty consequence.

This ideal world is the world of religion. This
is what the poetic needs of mankind have done
with facts and imaginings picked up almost at
random. Christianity, for instance, seized on
many harsh and grating notes, as well as on sweet
sounds, — the legends of Chaldæan shepherds, the
traditions of wandering sheiks, the chronicles of
barbarous chieftains, the rites of fanatical priests,
the prophecies of unpoised minds, as well as on
the story of a beautiful and holy life, rendered more
beautiful and holy by its remoteness from European experience, and on many another note, in
itself odd and seemingly unfit for religious use;

and out of them it has created a religion, which, with all its defects, is permeated with poetry. The figure of Christ, the image of Mary, the stories of the Apostolic age, the Gregorian chants, the Gothic cathedrals, the Divine Comedy, the vesper bells, are all parts of this irrational poetry. And the defects are for the greater part due to the practical minds who desire to bring these strange, incongruous elements into a rational union, — rational according to an unpoetic interpretation of the experiences of life. And if one says that Christianity is permeated with poetry rather than with truth, it is because truth is of two kinds: scientific truth, which is the accumulated experience of the senses, ranged and sorted according to reason; and poetic truth, which is the sorting and arrangement of recorded images (exalted and illumined by an emotional hunger as they dwell in the memory), in accordance with the poetic needs of mankind. One satisfies the mind, the other satisfies the soul. And as the soul is vague, elusive, uncertain, tremulous, and passionate, it has never yet, at least with the masses of men, accepted the conclusions of reason. Its values do not coincide with the values of reason. Its satisfactions do not tally with the satisfactions of reason. Therefore rationalism and religion do not agree. Religion can take strange symbols, strange doctrines, strange dogmas, at which the scientific mind stares with amazement — sin, redemption, an incarnate God, a Trinity, a heaven, and a hell; because for religion these things do not rank as rational facts: they are symbolic causes, the least unsatisfactory explanation for the emotions and imaginings of the soul; they are the least unsympathetic evasions of the question, *Why am I?*

One may criticise Christianity, one may find it irrational or transcending human experience in almost every detail, one may be repelled by its superstitions, dull to its poetry; but, on the other hand, one cannot be rational and create a new religion. Religion is an emotional assumption to explain the world of reason. Poor humanity, it cannot have all that it would like. In our present stage of knowledge, at least, an adequate expression of emotional life can only be through poetry and religion. Poetry and music, love and hope, life and death, these persuade men that religion, however formulated in superstition and irrational dogma, is near to Truth.

State contenti, umana gente, al *quia:*
chè, se potuto aveste veder tutto,
mestier non era partorir Maria.

CREDO QUIA POSSIBILE

I

THERE is something almost unfilial in the stolid indifference with which we pass by old Christian dogmas. Earnest generations thought, prayed, yearned, over their interpretation of the meaning of life, and fashioned dogmas which they believed would light the steps of their children and their children's children to endless generations, yet we scarce look to see what these dogmas may mean. Creeds of a thousand years are no more heeded than old letters garnered in the garret; yet it may happen that among those old yellowing sheets, franked and sealed, are love-letters which, however dull and childish they may seem to the fancy-free, rekindle old fires in the hearts of those who have loved and lost, or loved in vain.

The dogma-makers lived on our earth, they had faculties like ours, they loved and suffered, they were amazed and confounded; they, too, tried to discover a formula that should prove the key to the mystery of life. The same mystery that confronted them confronts us still. To some men

those old dogmas brought peace, self-mastery,
power; why may we not linger a little to examine
them ?

We are not free to use dogmas that postulate
facts inconsistent with the discoveries of science;
but science and religion have different duties.
Science seeks a formula that shall square with
human experience and satisfy the reason; religion
seeks a formula that shall minister to what in our
ignorance we call the soul's needs and quicken the
emotions. May we not find in the old dogmas
something not forbidden by science that may still
minister to the soul's needs ?

The Christian creed says, *Credo in Spiritum
Sanctum.* Is there nothing in human experience
to justify this dogma ? At one time in the
Middle Ages there was a sect of men who came
under the potent influence of this aspect of the
Godhead. They believed that to each Person of
the Trinity was allotted his period of divine
dominion. God the Father had had his reign,
God the Son was still reigning. Both reigns had
had their special characters, but neither had been
wholly adequate to the soul's needs, therefore there
was ground for hope that the Holy Ghost would
soon begin to reign, and that the season of children,
of lilies, of good men triumphant, was at hand.

Were not Abate Gioacchino del Fiore and his disciples right, in thinking that the hope of good tidings for the soul lay in worship of the Holy Spirit? The conception of God the Creator has its difficulties. The Beginning is the deep, permanent mystery; and the creation of a world in which pain and suffering mark every individual life, renders the claims of a Creator to man's gratitude very questionable. Also the idea that Jesus of Nazareth is God is very difficult. But when we turn toward the third Person, to that aspect of Deity which has never yielded to man's anthropomorphic needs, which at best has been represented by a dove, a bringer of peace, do we not discern more light?

II

We look through the telescope at night and see thousands upon thousands of suns, glorious in the surrounding dark. Their majesty inspires us with mingled feelings: fear before the vast unknown, reverence before the very great, exaltation at being a part of this mighty whole. But what, in the end, do we take away except bewilderment? There is no peace in the empyrean; there is turmoil, effort, energy. Do we perceive there the presence of God the Father or God the Son?

Yet if there is a Divine Spirit, how fit a working-place is this majestic universe for its incessant toil.

We look through the microscope; physicists, chemists, biologists, pry into the inner recesses of matter, only to find energy — everywhere, in the egg, in spermatozoa, in the minutest particles of matter, animal, vegetable, or inorganic, — restless energy, eternal effort. If we turn to the history of past life upon our globe, what do we find but records of energy, whether physical, chemical, or of that seemingly peculiar form which marks living organisms, everywhere energy leaving its trace in innumerable forms. In this history of life, according to our human standards, there has been a long procession, in which the principle of organic life, from the earliest period of vegetable existence, has advanced through manifold forms, upward, upward, in the depths of the sea, in the air, on land, by devious routes and strange passages, up, up, to the fish, to the bird, to four-footed beasts, and finally to man. Gradually, steadily, those mysterious forces which determine the nature of things, have been shaping gases and solids, crystals, drops of water, the pistil and stamens of the plant, the heart, lungs, eye, hand, and brain of man. In all organic life there are cells in restless energy; cells piled on cells, cells in many kinds of combinations, all taking shape according to the will of some strenuous, persistent, experimenting force. The cells of the clover arrange themselves to fashion the flower which shall secrete honey, the cells of the bee to create an insect which shall gather it, the cells of the man to form a creature with an appetite for that honey and also with a yearning to find something divine in the universe. Everywhere that man can peer he finds energy intent upon changing all that is into new forms. This process, different as it looks in the very large and in the very small, in distant stars, in the tides of ocean, in the flora, in sea creatures or in mammals, seems to be one and the same, proceeding through myriad forms of activity, always seeking to effect a change.

If this seeming is true, if all our world, all our universe, is the workroom, or playground it may be, for the same energy, may we not judge it, must we not judge it, by the only part of the pattern that is open to our judgment, by human life within our experience? How can corporeal creatures like ourselves, busily at work turning food into living tissue, entertain but the most remote understanding of elementary gases? What do we know of the ambitions, the enthusi-

asms, the discouragement, of coral insects? All
things that are, seem to be made of the same elements which, by their physico-chemical energy
after infinite experiments, have given to the
human brain consciousness; but we, who are the
products of happier combinations, cannot understand these same potential energies compounded
in lower forms. We must judge the whole process
by ourselves, by man. This is the inner meaning
of the saying, Know thyself. If we know ourselves, we shall know all.

If, then, this universal process, when we see it
at work in the only matters intelligible to us, in
ourselves, seems to be an effort to rise, to attain
the better, to bring the nobler to birth, — seems
to be a struggle to renounce the lower and mount
to a higher plane, — must we not suppose that the
laborious energies at work throughout the universe
are striving to do the same? Let us look at bits
of the pattern that we may perceive what is the
design. Take a mother whose life is in her son's
life, whose thoughts are all of him, whose hopes
are his, who dotes upon his happiness; bid her
choose for him between a higher life linked with
pain and sorrow, and a lower life loaded with
pleasures and worldly success, and will she hesi-
tate? The upward energy that works through

all her being will not let her choose a lower plane
for her son.

> Fatti non foste a viver come bruti,
> ma per seguir virtute e conoscenza.

Take the son of such a mother at a time when,
young blood flowing through his veins, he has
fallen in love. The law of all organic nature is,
Be fruitful and multiply. The tree bears fruit,
the vines bring forth grapes, the herring spawns,
the lioness bears her cubs; all creatures obey the
great command, all hand on the miraculous torch
of life. But the young lover sees deeper into the
heart of things:

> I struggle towards the light; and ye
> Once long'd-for storms of love!
> If with the light ye cannot be,
> I bear that ye remove.

He hears the pulsing reverberations of the animal
command; and he hears also commands less
audible, yet to his soul still more imperious.
He must consecrate himself to the highest, he *must*,
even if he is compelled to turn his back on all the
happiness that looks so fair before him, the sweet
blue eyes, " the soft, enkerchief'd hair." Here,
in the mother's heart, in the young man's heart,
where life beats at its fastest, the need of breaking

free from the lower is most peremptory. Such is
the pattern wrought by this energy as it appears
in human life. Biologists call this force blind,
but to the ignorant it seems to see its path " as
birds their trackless way."

III

What can we infer of this universal energy but
that it is working to change what is into something
higher ?   All this turmoil, this commotion of earth
and heavens, is a discontent, and a struggle. May
we not here see, in this endeavor to supplant the
lower by the higher, a Holy Spirit at work ?

What the source or origin of the universe may
be lies beyond human guessing; but there seems
to be an imprisoned power struggling to detach
itself from base integuments, striving to dominate
some hindering medium, aspiring to make the
universe anew.   Matter, or whatever we call the
substance of the phenomena on which our consciousness has dawned, however far from any
apparent sympathy with man, however muddy
its vesture, however hideous its aspect, is under
the control of some energy, which displays itself
in heat, light, motion, thought, and love.   Even
if the proper dogmatic adjective for this energy
is *physico-chemical,* may not the adjective *divine*

be appropriate also? What limit can human foresight assign to its achievements? And as we watch this energy at work in what seems to us our best and noblest, may we not infer that love is the medium in which this upward impulse finds the least impediment, the least hinderance to its free motions; or, differently put, that love is the highest expression of the universal force which, everywhere and without ceasing, is striving to create a universe of a higher order?

It sounds arrogant and foolish for man to make himself the measure of the universe, to assert that his thoughts and acts are the fruit and crown of things; but he has no choice. He seeks everywhere, and finds nothing that he can call higher or nobler than the expression of this energy in good men. And there can be no more solemn or admonishing sanction for high endeavor than the knowledge that we are the standard-bearers of the divine spirit. It is ennobling to think that if we advance our standards, the divine advances; if we fall back, by so much the divine loses in the battle; that the divine energy manifesting itself in us is one with the energy that whirls the stolid worlds.

Is not this the Holy Spirit that Abate Gioacchino dimly apprehended? Is not this the force

that dawned, as in a dream, upon the consciousness of those mystics who have felt a conviction
that they were face to face with God? By some
favoring juncture of circumstances these holy
men suddenly became sensitive to the meaning of
the cosmic process, and their souls cried out, Lo,
God is here! Is not that which we call prayer
the unconscious bending of ourselves to act in
concord with this universal energy, as heliotropic
plants turn to the light? This potential element
in the stuff that composes our universe has been
able to evolve a lover's abnegation, a mother's
devotion, it has created the imagination of a
Shakspere, it moves to music, and clothes itself
in light; surely it is divine. Would it be higher
or holier if we could hear the rush of Cherubim or
see the gleam upon a Seraph's wings?

Man cannot hope, within his narrow compass of
sense, to feel the fulness of the divine spirit.
He cannot open his soul wide enough to comprehend what this universal endeavor is, seemingly
infinite in extent, infinite in patience, infinite in
perseverance. But if of the divine we demand
heroism in the face of danger, has there not been,
even in the contracted limits of human history,
heroism sufficient? If of the divine we demand
suffering, we have but to let our thoughts rest

for an instant upon the long ages of animal life upon this globe, one long track of blood, in order to shudder at the cruelty endured.

Is not this struggle of the higher against the lower, whether under the waters of ocean, in pre-glacial jungles, or in our own hearts, as wonderful and splendid as the conflict of Michael and the host of heaven against the rebellious angels? Surely, yes.

Suppose that man is the highest life in all the universe, suppose that his race and all animal life is doomed to destruction as our planet cools off, is it not better to have endeavored and suffered than never to have endeavored at all? Possibly, somewhere, a memory may live of how the human race rose from bestiality and lust to devotion to beauty, truth, and love. But even if no memory of man shall continue after he has perished, still, throughout the universe, the restless energy that animated him will continue undaunted, making its experiments, striving to change that which is into that which, according to our human judgment, shall be better. Is not this a Divine Spirit, whether it works through visible, tangible, ponderable things, or through spiritual essences; whether it be an archangel or physico-chemical activity that has created the soul of man?

Is not this the aspect of the Trinity that must, as the disciples of Joachim believed, outlive its other aspects, and do most to satisfy the yearning desire of man to find something holy in the universe ? May we not all repeat : *Credo in Spiritum Sanctum ?*

ON BEING ILL

THERE are, according to the poet, "four seasons
in the mind of man"; and each has its appropriate mood, its range of vision, its philosophy.
But, in addition to these four seasons, there are
two other categories which shift a man's thoughts,
the object of his vision and his philosophy, even
more than the change from Spring to Summer
or from Autumn to Winter. These other categories are health and sickness. In these two
states man beholds two very different worlds;
so different are these worlds, that if a man should
live in one only, he would know but half the
human universe.

Health is the normal state. In it the faculties
are in equilibrium and fulfil their obvious duties.
Upon it, as if it was a sure foundation, science
builds hypotheses and dogmas, and men of
action with a turn for literature construct what
they call a sane and happy philosophy of life.
Health is the condition of life's daily routine.
Health accepts life as a matter of course, without

demur, without criticism, almost without appreciation. A healthy man is indifferent to all theories about the universe; one theory is as good as another. He himself is the centre of his universe; and his senses, like so many radii, describe its uttermost bounds.

Suppose the healthy man to be a farmer. Then the prime interests of his life will cluster around his barn, his cowshed and his vegetable garden. His affections embrace his potato hillocks, his purpling cabbages, and the corn-patch, where in July the stately stalks deck their heads with plumes and outdo in parallel symmetry the spears of Velasquez' conquering Spaniards at Breda. Here is his universe — house, barn, woodpile, chicken run, pump, orchard and meadows — what to him are the outlying regions beyond the farm limits? How is he concerned with fields and woodland across the county turnpike, with countries over seas, or with the ethereal distances that encompass our solar system? Health has fixed the bourns of his intellectual kingdom. Its axis is in the stable, and all the cloud-capped hypotheses that science with infinite industry has built up concerning what lies between his boundary line and the farthest regions of infinite space, count

for less than the humming of the teakettle or
the cackle of the hens. All attempts by Science
or Philosophy to shift the central point of his
universe to some part of the Milky Way, or to
the Absolute, must fail. And yet it is upon the
healthy man, upon the reports of his senses,
upon the processes of his reason, that science
builds its truths, and philosophy its hypotheses.

The business of a healthy man is to live his
life; and in order to live it well, he must make
himself, so far as he can, a creature of instinct,
if possible an automaton. He adores the god
of action, because health is, in its manifestations,
a mere bundle of activities. Love of action is
the patriotism of health. This attitude toward
life gives a comfortable sense of snugness, of
familiarity, of home, and protects such as adopt
it against the vast outer universe that serves, it
seems, but to confuse and dismay them. It
holds a man's attention fast to the region where
he fills his belly, chooses his wife, digs, hoes,
drives his cows afield and calls them back to the
milking. This attitude is natural, human; it
proclaims man's origin. But in the opinion of
those who care for unrestricted liberty of speculation and imagining, it deprives the human mind
of its noblest birthright. For them it is high

treason to what should be man's governing
principle. Nevertheless, action remains the basis
of life; and, as even the most sceptical critic
must admit, action renders a service that might
well seem to compensate for all the limitations
which it imposes upon the human spirit. Action
makes a theatre out of life.

If we were to weigh with even hand one by one
the good and evil things that fate lays in the
balances, in order to determine whether human
life be worth the living, perhaps none of the
things deemed good — not the luxuriant vitality
of youth, not affection, nor romantic love, not
interest in work, nor the approbation of our
fellows — would weigh as heavily as the pleasure
got from the theatre of life. The drama of life
is unintermittent, boundless in resource; of
infinite variety, it appeals to every taste. It
reckons up its actors by the million. It dresses
up in royal robes, with crowns, sceptres, and all
the wardrobe of imperial millinery, kings and
emperors, moves them about, and causes them
to utter majestic harangues, and pirouette over
the stage in a manner to rivet our amazed attention. It takes bandits, pirates, cossacks,
and parades them to and fro to a wild music.
And these are but supernumeraries who fill in

the background and the wings of the stage. A little in front of them come players, whose names are printed on the programme, enumerated as statesmen, philosophers, poets, musicians, explorers, and so on. Finally, in front of them all, come the protagonists in Everyman's drama — the household headed by the cook, the milkman, and the butcher's boy, the immediate neighbors (each separate group playing its own comedy within the great comedy), husband and wife, nursery maid and babies, schoolboys and tutors, guests, cousins, callers, and all the multitude who fill the minor rôles, the chauffeur, the trolley-car conductor, the old lady who in times of illness comes to advise mental healing, the elderly clerk, the lazy office-boy, the fashionable tailor, the cobbler round the corner, the habitué at the club, the fruit-vender, the policeman, the parson's assistant, the political reformer. The theatre of life with its tragedy, comedy, farce, its gruesome scenes and its delightful episodes, has but one patent fault; it has no plot and no apparent meaning. Healthy men, the rich, the pious, praise both plot and meaning; but the indifferent spectator can distinguish neither, nothing but eternal motion. A rational explanation of action is that in providing the theatre of life it

furnishes the justification of life. All living
things are actors who keep on going in order that
scene shall follow scene without intermission;
for this men preserve their own lives, for this
they rear children, future actors, who shall take the
places of those whose parts are ended. "All the
world's a stage, and all the men and women merely
players," but men and women are also spectators. All are admitted to the show; some sit
in the orchestra stalls, some in the upper gallery.
At one and the same time all men are both players
and spectators; they may be mute supernumeraries in the noisier parts of the drama, but all are
protagonists of some particular episode. All this
we owe to action, and action is the product of health.

Action, then, keeps life alive and furnishes a
nonpareil theatre. To the eyes of the healthy
man this theatre is delightful and life an invalu-
able possession. This is the mood of health.

II

Once a man is ill, the scene changes. All that
great stretch of universe that formerly reached
out, in dusky dimness, from beyond the farm
road toward infinity, has sunk below the horizon,
it has become as if it had never been. The field
of corn, the potato patch, the flower garden,

the gravelled walk, the porch, have also become part of uncharted darkness, merged into chaos; even hall, stairway, the whole house outside the sickroom door, is now beyond the further edge of twilight consciousness. The sick man's physical universe has shrunk to a bedroom, it is circumscribed by four narrow walls, but it serves all the purposes of the mightiest universe, it fills his thoughts, and presents those marks of order and intelligibility that distinguish the tract within the intellectual reach of the human mind from whatever may lie beyond. It has advantages over any larger universe in that the smaller it is, the more intelligible, the more home-like it becomes, and in that it stands more clearly in definite relations to the sick man's inner self.

The central point of interest is his bed. The white coverlet lies like new-fallen snow. Under it his legs, two long projections with which he appears to have little or nothing to do, stretch away down towards the foot of the bed, like mountain ranges on a map of physical geography; while the light covering falls away in gentle slopes on either side. Then the brass bedpost catches his eye. It draws to itself more than its share of light, and, as if the words *Fiat Lux* had been spoken directly to it, radiates brazenly.

But an object near by, on the table at the foot of the bed, is far more interesting. A long green stalk rises from a yellow vase, and stands very tall and straight in its pride at carrying the perfect flower that, with its snowy petals half disclosed, half folded as if to hold their fragrance in, crowns the green stem. This white rose is a triumphant issue of the efforts of Nature, of her experiments in valley and meadow, in sunshine and in shade, the achievement of the noble collaboration of root and stalk, of leaves and blossoms.

If Nature had aimed to produce color only, or fragrance only, it would be seemingly intelligible that man should chance to be pleased by the color or by the fragrance; but according to what doctrine of chances should a man be charmed not only by the color and the fragrance, but also by the exquisite texture of the petals that fits them for no rougher office than to line a fairy's cradle? Each petal opens at the touch of light, and then, as if the caress of the full sunlight were too poignant, covers itself with shadows and half-tones.

In a state of health one accepts a rose as part of the great adventure, not less wonderful, nor more, than all the other elements that go to

make up that adventure. But the mind, half
set free from the emaciated body, cannot take
the rose merely so. Why is it that Milton
plants roses thick in his Garden of Eden; why
does Dante make the saints and angels of God
but petals in the vast rose of the heaven of
heavens? Why is there never a lover that does
not compare his mistress to a rose? Can it be
by chance that the rose and the soul of man
are matched so melodiously? And as the rose
has travelled along its vegetable path, trusting
to the wind or to the honey bee for transporta-
tion to a kindlier soil, is it *chance* that has conferred upon her this combination of color,
fragrance and texture, and brought her as it
were to a trysting place with the soul of man,
who, on his part, having traced his way through
millions of years down a dark path, has attained
the senses that are ravished by that union of
color, fragrance, and texture? What service has
the rose rendered to our ancestors that we should
admire it beyond all rational measure? Did it
feed them, clothe them, warm them, or serve to
deck some otherwise unattractive maid and win
for her a wooer? Did our ancestors, whether
beasts or human progenitors of retreating skull
and tusklike teeth, breathe in its beauty and

take fresh courage for the battle of life? Can it be by *chance* that man has come to find in a flower the great symbol of Beauty? Why is not the fruit more beautiful to him than the flower? Why not the vegetable than the fruit? Why not the fish than the vegetable, or a lamb chop most beautiful of all? The rose does not help the human being, even to-day, in the struggle for life; rather she is a hinderance. She stands there in the vase, and as the sick man's delighted eye follows the contour of leaf and petal, and dwells upon the dainty setting of the corolla in the calyx (as if the soul of a bird had alighted on the soul of a nest), she asserts: "To gaze on Beauty is the nobleness of life." Is this *chance?* Or is there some element in the spirit of man that renders him as he proceeds upon his upward journey more sensitive to beauty, and, as time goes on, will cause him to perceive beauty lying thick about him, in flower, leaf, pebble, waterdrop, in every clod of common earth, and so at last establish harmonious relations between him and all that is? Is this the end to which Life consciously aspires, the argument to justify creation and existence?

To the spirit, still uncertain of long sojourn in its fleshly dress, the beauty of the rose is a tor-

menting riddle. The spirit keeps asking : "Why,
why am I imprisoned in this compound of dust,
condemned to suffer when this insensible machine
goes wrong ? What whimsical power commanded
me, a spirit, to be conscious of physical malad-
justment ?" And the rose keeps answering :
"You are also conscious of me."

Is knowledge of the rose a piece of mystical
experience, a communion with a symbol of pure
beauty, a partial and momentary loss of self in
the consciousness of that which is Life's explanation ? The mystics, bound by the words and
phrases of human experience, use images of
light, of sound, of sweetness; but in all they
say, they merely try to express what the rose
is to the sick man. Is every sick man a mystic ?
Does illness dilapidate the blocks of physical
dogma out of which is built the edifice of daily
life ? Does it dissolve the mortar of the matter-
of-fact, dispel the illusions of habitual action,
and leave the soul face to face with symbols of
something toward which all life aspires ?

III

A little beyond the foot of the bed come the
fireplace and mantlepiece. The small dimensions
of the room leave but a narrow passage for a

white-capped, white-aproned, ministrant, who walks to and fro with noiseless steps, and, when the clock strikes the hour, brings a spoonful of some medicinal potion which custom, or fashion, or hope, foists upon the sick. The wood fire preaches mortality, as it resolves into their elements the logs of oak, chestnut, and birch which cost nature so much pains to endow with life. But another symbol withdraws the wandering eye from the fire. On the mantlepiece, leaning against the wall, there is a rude picture, painted on copper in archaic, Flemish style. The subject is the crucifixion. At the foot of the cross Mary stands erect, John with bowed head close by, and hovering in the air little truncated cherubs catch in golden chalices the drops of blood that fall from the dead Christ's wounds. At first one jumps to the conclusion that this scene, acknowledged throughout Christendom as the supreme human tragedy, has been always misunderstood. The minds of men have been preoccupied by the ecclesiastical interpretation, which regards the Crucified Christ as the centre of the tragedy, and puts at the climax of its litany, "By Thy cross and passion." The spectacle of physical suffering, especially to men in health, wrings the corporeal sensibility, and in the case of finely

tuned natures even imprints imitative marks in
hands, and feet and side; and yet a far deeper
suffering was endured at the foot of the cross.
Mary is the centre of the tragedy:

> Stabat mater dolorosa
> juxta crucem lacrimosa,
>   dum pendebat filius.
> Cujus animam gementem
> contristantem et dolentem
>   pertransivit gladius.

The poet knew that the mother was the greater
sufferer, for a sword had also pierced his soul.
She, who had stored up in her heart all the words
of her little boy, all the sayings of her eldest
son, her beautiful youth, her divine leader of
men, suffered more pain than nails or lance have
power to inflict. Nevertheless Mary is not the
centre of the tragedy. Christendom is right;
instinctively it feels that the figure on the cross
is the cynosure of human interest.

The crucifixion is a tragedy, not because it
represents human pain, even pain undeserved,
but because the cross passionately asserts a
truth at the heart of life. There, on the cross,
hangs a body, worshipped by Christendom as
the body of one who in himself incorporated
both the human and the divine. This belief

gives a superhuman poignancy to the crucifixion. The belief in this union of man and God in Christ crucified is true, not because God came down from his celestial throne to earth, but because man is the highest exponent of the mysterious force that pulses through the universe, the clearest evidence of divinity. Why should we care whether the divine is human, when there is such abundant witness that the human is divine, in all that we demand of the divine? In heroism, in self-sacrifice, in the power of loving?

To the sick man the divine reveals itself in many a way, it fills his sickroom. He does not ask that angels shall minister to him, for woman's hands smooth his pillow, bring him a marvellous beverage, called milk, and a delicate, transparent, glittering mass of bubbles that dance in rainbow colors within the tumbler; this ambrosia the prosaic nurse calls whipped up white of egg, as if by mere words she could exorcise the spirit of poetry. Poetry invades the sickroom, it sings in the sunbeams, it leaps with the leaping flames of the fire, and snuggles in the bosom of the rose. Poetry is but the harbinger of the divine, and both express themselves in the human voice. If the forces of life can take the dust of the earth and compound it into a woman's hands,

and that miracle does not convince us that the
forces of life are divine, then no other miracles
or revelations will.

The divine manifests itself in beauty, in poetry,
in light, in the rose, in human affections. But in
order to manifest itself the divine must first
exist; and the crucifixion testifies that that
which is potentially divine can only become
divine through pain. This is the teaching of
the crucifixion, and this is more readily set forth
for the multitude by obvious symbols of nails
and spear thrust, than in the mother's woe.
The crucifixion is the supreme allegory of the
triumph of the divine through pain, the symbol
that divinity is the child of pain, and only by
the ministration of pain comes to birth.

It may be that pain is a process of purification,
of rarefaction of the spirit, and so enables the
spirit's more ethereal part to rise, leaving behind
that which clogs and impedes its flight. This
doctrine has long been held with respect to man,
— *patiendo fit homo melior*, — and, inasmuch as
man is but an integral part of all the universe,
how can a law be true for him if it be not also
true for all the universe ? All the nervous system
— if the answer is to be looked for in the colloca-
tion of cells — has come into being in order to

increase life, to enlarge it, to render it more sensitive. Why, if the vibrations that cause consciousness of sound, sight, touch, smell, warmth,
and the rest, are creating mind, or enabling mind
to possess a local habitation, and if pain hovers
about these vibrations, as a mother hovers about
her children, and if the sterner tempering of
character is wrought by pain, what can we do
but acknowledge that pain is mysteriously at
work around, above, and below us, guiding, warn-
ing, chastising, blessing, using the mind of man
as material for its high purpose of creating the
divine ?

This is but the humdrum attempt of the well
man to express in words the thoughts that haunted
him when sick. While he lay in bed, he did not
need the intervention of words. To the sick
man words are gross, palpable things, they come
with footfall heavier than that of the choreman
who fetches wood for the fire ; and each word,
like a traveller from regions of ice and snow, is
wrapped in all sorts of outer garments that
conceal the thought within. They disturb the
quiet of the room ; they distort and caricature
the fine Ariels of thought that hover just outside
the portals of comprehension, and would come
in, were words delicate enough not to travesty

H

them. Thoughts crowd about, eager to explain, longing to tell the sick man why it is that pain is his benefactor, and when they pass through the gates of comprehension, and are stuffed into words, they are no longer Ariels, but mummers that gesticulate, make faces, and mock the listener. This is the vexation the sick man endures; he feels that he has been lifted to purer regions, closer to the meaning that for him, at least, lies hidden behind symbols, — behind the crucifix, the rose, a woman's hand, behind light, behind love, — and yet he can never remember, after he has returned to earth, just what he really experienced and believed.

But if he turns his attention from that which he vainly hopes to find in the wallet of his memory — you cannot fetch home light in a bag — to what is really there, he finds religion. Then, at last, he realizes what sickness is doing for him. The healthy man has no time for religion; he is concerned with action. He must plough his field, sow his corn, hoe his potatoes, and trail the honeysuckle over the trellis. His mind is busy with manifold occupations, hopes, and anxieties. The theatre of life, filling the stage of his universe, takes what leisure he may have. Or, if he has a religion, it is either an inheritance,

like his grandfather's clothes fitted for a man of
different stature, or one which he has constructed
out of fears of the evil that may befall, or out of
gratitude for evil escaped. The sick man is in
quite a different case. His stage is shrunk to
his bedroom; his drama observes the unities.
But for the dumb presence of the nurse, he is
alone, alone with the white rose, with the picture
of the crucifixion, with his body and the hovering
spirits of life and death. His drama has become
as simple as that of Æschylus, and he drifts off
into the religious mood, a mood of humble curiosity concerning life, and of quest for a loyalty
which shall assert his need of holiness to be
proof that his soul has received an imprint, no
matter how faint, from the presence of something
holy.

The first feeling is of curiosity. What is this
life that floats, like the Ark, upon a waste of
inanimate turbulence?   Everywhere motion,
everywhere restlessness.   Is it only in this chance
combination of cells, the brain, that consciousness can make her dwelling-place? And does
my consciousness merely reflect for a time the multitudinous outside world, like the surface of a
pool, and then, as when the water sinks away
into the sands beneath, reflect no more? Is it

all mere *chance* — the white rose, the crucifixion,
the Son nailed to the cross, the mother in agony
upon the ground beneath? Were these things
caused by chance, or are there forces that have
a purpose and tend towards an end, in whose
obedience a man may range himself, and spend
himself in an effort to achieve? Is there a soul of
the universe with which his soul can confederate?

IV

How shall a man go about to find the soul of
the universe? What shibboleth, what badge,
shall he look for? What do we mean by holiness? Is it a mere series of resignations, the
bidding farewell one after another to the impulses
of life, to the desires of the body and the mind?
is it the shaking off as much as may be of all
corporeal control? Or, is it an abstraction de-
duced from the higher pleasures of life, from
heroism, from the exultations of sacrifice, from
the joy of pure thought? Or do our souls come
into touch, as our earth's atmosphere touches
the ethereal space beyond, with an oversoul, and
become hallowed by that communion? Or, is
the upward flight of the soul of necessity in and
through a region that, by its mere remoteness
from the friction of life, inspires the human

spirit with a calm, a cool, a peace, and an exaltation ?

Cut off from all action, floating down a stream of incoherent thoughts, the sick man comes to feel that he has had an experience of holiness, like a pilgrim who has visited some far off sanctuary. His sick room has become a shrine. Here he has been alone, face to face, with the one question that to him is real — all other questions, all other aspects of things, all perplexities, having been swallowed up in the night of chaos beyond the limits of his sickroom universe.

Illness is one of the great privileges of life. It denies the common value of things, and whispers that man's destiny is bound up with transcendental powers. Illness pares and lops off the outer parts of life and leaves us with the essence of it. That essence gropes blindly for its fundamental relationships. Is this consciousness of mine, — which becomes, when shrunk to its inmost being, a mere spiritual hunger for union with something other than itself, an isolated drop of what was once an ocean of being ? Does it imply that a universal soul has disintegrated, that all its constituent elements have been broken up and scattered, each still impressed with the memory that they were once parts of a whole ? Or is this hunger but a sign of a new awakening, the first movement towards a combination, a union, that shall be divine?

Is there a Creator? Or, is the idea of a Creator the product of superstitious ignorance, which has subdued the human soul and too lightly applied the human analogy of man reshaping matter? Who would willingly admit a Creator that had created this universe, with all its suffering, unless upon the supposition that He was so cramped by fate or dearth of material, that He could only create it of warring forces and dragons' teeth? But who can conceive that mechanical forces, in the course of myriad encounters with one another, have by mere accident struck out the sparks of mind?

And why this eternal commotion? Is all this turmoil the struggle of a baser element to attain self-realization, to achieve psychic life? Is the whole universe seeking more life and fuller? Or is life our original sin, and death the great purifier? Is it beneficent death that is striving to cast out the vexing seeds of life, and restore a universal calm? Is death the great ocean of peace to which all the rivers of existence flow? Is the blotting out of the universe beyond the farm road, the reduction of it to a small sickroom, the diminution of the innumerable *dramatis persona* to one white-capped, white-aproned nurse, a sample of the divine effort towards simplicity and peace? Is consciousness the real ill? Is this universal commotion harmless till consciousness arises? Is life a privilege, a duty, or a sin? Why should our ripples disturb the peace of God?

While these fancies come and go, there stands the picture of the crucifixion, there the white rose opens its petals wider hour by hour as if it would enfold the world in the arms of its fragrance. The one proclaims that there is a greater nobleness in pain than the inanimate is capable of, and the other asks: "What but a beneficent force could create a white rose or a child?" How can one answer them? These are witnesses that life is nobler than death. The human heart does beat quicker at the sight of a will to suffer, it does rejoice at roses. If the propulsive rhythm of the universe has produced these as samples of its purposes, as intimations of its goal, does not the whole pattern of existence suddenly seem to burst out as if written in letters of light? Right and wrong cease to be meaningless terms; a way opens to act in unison with the motions of the universe, to help, no matter in

how trivial a respect, its upward will to prevail;
the music of hope blows in the wind, sings in
April showers, murmurs in the mysterious noises
of the woods, in the voices of men, in the anguish
of the crucifix, and calls upon life to feel, to enjoy, and to suffer, for the sake of more life.

In this way the sick man's thoughts go to and
fro. The drama of life has simplified itself into
a mystery play. Life parleys with Death. Death
urges peace :

> Ease after toil, port after stormy seas,
> Peace after war, death after life, doth greatly please.

But in the soft, caressing insistence upon the
pleasantness of peace, how can we tell whether
the attraction that draws us on to lie stiller and
stiller, is a summing up of all the arguments that
belittle life and extol death, or a mere self-indulgence of the body, counselling ease ? Does
this sweetly magical incantation, under which
the limbs lie quiet and the hands involuntarily
clasp themselves on the breast, come from the
body or the mind ? And is remembrance of
happy days, is the pleading of old maxims that
condemn a physical surrender to death, is the
desire to worship a god of the living, a mere
psychical mechanism set in motion by the heart,

beating rhythmically to the oscillations that run through the physical universe? It is all a religious mystery play. Life is religious, Death is religious. The question, "Shall I live or shall I die," resolves itself into a question of loyalty. Is life or death our God?

V

The return from illness to health is like coming up from a dive, supposing the time from when the swimmer first sees light through the water until his head rises to the surface to be the affair of weeks. The change in physical condition may be slow, but the change in orientation takes place in a twinkling and is complete. The eye no longer looks down into unplumbed deeps, but back toward the light of day; curiosity for the ultimate yields to a golden memory of familiar things, — friends, household goods, books, barking dogs, the freshness of grass and trees. The body has reasserted itself. The dreaming imagination is dragged away from its goal by the galloping senses. Eye, ear, touch, taste, start upon a rampage. Especially does the appetite for food wax furious, discovering itself endowed with power to transform a coddled egg into something rich and strange, and to illumine chicken broth with a charm that no art can equal. The universe, lately shrunk to the sickroom, now rises again, like the Genie out of the bottle in which he had been imprisoned; the sickroom becomes a house of detention, and at its door, as in a seashell clapped to the ear, the convalescent hearkens to all the rumours of the outer world.

It is the very completeness of the body's triumph that constitutes the weakness of its permanent victory. The exultation with which it mocks the dreamy imagination is too plainly the work of recovering nerves, of reinvigorated muscles, of hungry physical organs. It is a triumph of force, not of reason. Health is not magnanimous; it prosecutes its victory relentlessly, as if it feared to leave a single dreamy thought unquenched. Its victory proves nothing except that we are living things. Perhaps the dead rejoice in death, as greatly as the living do in life.

Convalescence, however, is a pleasant time. Away with Thomas-à-Kempis, Obermann, Amiel, away with anchorites and monks, bats that haunt the chill vaults of the antechamber of Death.

> Come, thou goddess fair and free,
> In heaven yclept Euphrosyne!

The sick man on his path back to life has a vora-
cious appetite for the humour, the gayety, the
light follies of life. He bids the nurse take away
the Bible and *Paradise Lost*, which during his
dark days he had kept at his elbow; he asks for
*Punch, Pickwick, La Rôtisserie de la Reine Pédau-
que, Don Quixote*. Mirth, even in its ruder
livery, appears as the most desirable of human
emotions. Falstaff comes habited in a magical
radiance, as if jollity were humanity's noblest
attribute. And, indeed, if the partisans of health
are right, there is no very good reason for supposing that it is not.

The convalescent's ears crave the crowing of
the cock, the cluck of hens, the grunt of pigs;
even the expletives of the passing teamster sound
with a rough music, chiming in with the universal
chorus of the world's noises that sing a pæan in
praise of life.

Life seizes upon every means of appeal within
its power to lure the sick man back from the
worship of death. There is something almost
comic in its solicitude lest it should lose one
adorer. No coquette — not Beatrice nor Cé-
limène — ever took such pains, adjusted ribbons,
ringlets, ruffles, lifted or dropped her eyes, turned
a slim neck, or smiled or sighed, with a tithe of

the flirtatiousness of life. Each man fancies
himself an Antony, and the spirit of Life, a very
Cleopatra, head over heels enamoured of him;
he yields unconditionally to her bewitching lure.

At last the nurse goes, the doctor takes his
leave, the medicine bottles are put on the closet
shelf, the patient is up and about, and then,
thoroughly subdued to the humours of Life, —
for Life is April when it woos, December when it
weds — he is turned out of doors, back to the
dull daily routine, back to hoeing, ploughing,
weeding, back to haggling, buying and selling,
back to the world of living men.   Life, the Circe,
who looked so fair, has bewitched him, metamor-
phosed him from a spirit into an animal, put her
collar on him and turned him loose, to run on all
fours like other animals after the things that
seem to him desirable.

Even then, in moments of leisure, in twilight
intervals between the work of day and the hours
of sleep, or, when on a starry night he leans forth
from his window, as St. Augustine and Monica
leaned from the window of their inn at Ostia
to brood over the text, "Enter thou into the joy
of thy Lord," — in such moments he broods upon
the thoughts that swept over him when sick, and
he muses upon the strangeness of life and wonders

whether he did not see more clearly with his heavy eyes, and apprehend more clearly with his fevered brow, when he lay upon the bed in his sickroom, than now when busy with the rough activities of life.

VI

THE HOUSE OF SORROW

Prologue

The traveller looked about him. The glorious sunlight of the preceding day had gone; the glittering greenery that had frolicked with the breeze was no longer to be seen. The trees along the roadside were gnarled, stunted, sombre; the bushes were scarcely more than brambles. Bleakness covered everything. Grass, such as it was, showed itself only in patches; the soil was stony, the air chill.

The traveller wrapped his cloak about him. Whether his senses were sharpened by the dreariness of his surroundings, or whether they instinctively sought a new object for their attention, he could not say; but be became aware, gradually, — as a sound sleeper slowly wakes to the things about his bed, — of some one beside him, travelling the same way, taking, it seemed, even steps with himself. He felt no surprise, but rather as

if he were picking up a memory that had been
lying just under the surface of consciousness, —
as if he ought to have known that some one had
been beside him for an indefinite time.

The traveller walked on for a while in silence;
and then, overcome half by curiosity, half by a
mixture of resentment and suspicion, turned and
demanded a little curtly where the other was
going.

"I am going your way," replied the stranger,
and the two walked on together, side by side.

"I beg your pardon," said the traveller, "but I
know, as I am immersed in my own thoughts,
that I cannot be an acceptable companion. We
had better journey singly; I will go ahead or fall
behind, as you choose."

"I prefer to keep even pace," answered the
other.

Hardly knowing whether or not to be offended,
the traveller hesitated; should he go ahead or fall
behind? But, though he could not tell why, he
did neither; he kept on the same road at the same
pace, step by step, with his companion.

The landscape grew still more desolate; the
earth seemed hostile to vegetable life. A rare
tree, here and there, shook its barren branches;
prickly things rendered the walking difficult.

The traveller thought to himself: "I will turn round and go back, and so I shall both leave this detestable place and escape from this importunate companion."

The stranger spoke up: "No, let us keep on together."

The traveller started, and making a feeble attempt to smile, said, "You seem to be a mind-reader." He decided to stop at once; nevertheless he continued to keep on the same road at the same pace. Then he thought, forgetting that he had not spoken aloud, "It was not polite in me to let him know that I wished to shake myself free of his company. I will quietly turn off to the right or left."

"No, let us keep on the same road," repeated the stranger.

At this the traveller contained himself no longer, but burst out, almost angrily, "Who are you?"

"I am the Spirit of Life," answered the other; "you and I are journeying together."

The traveller did not understand what the stranger meant; but he was aware of a bitter chill in the air and of still greater desolation all about, and he determined to cast manners to the wind and run for it; but no, his feet kept on the same way, at the same pace.

"Be not impatient," said his companion, "this is our road."

The chill struck through the traveller's cloak, his fingers trembled with cold, but he kept on. As they crossed the brow of a low hill they saw a great, gloomy building lying before them. The traveller thought of fortresses and prisons in foreign lands that he had read of.

"I shall turn here and go back," he cried, amazed at the foolish terror of his imagination.

"We must go on," replied the stranger.

They were now close under the shadow of the building.

"What is this abhorrent place?" asked the traveller.

"This," answered his companion, taking the traveller's arm, "is the House of Sorrow."

The traveller felt a sword pierce his heart, yet his footsteps did not fail; for, against his will, the Spirit of Life bore him up. He went on with even step, and the two crossed the threshold.

I

They that have experienced a great sorrow are born again. The world they are now in is quite different from their old world. In that earlier world they lived upon terms of household familiar-

I

ity with Joy and Felicity; now they must lie down
by the side of Sorrow and eat with Sorrow beside
them at the board.   Outward things may assert
their identity to eye, to ear, to touch, but outward
things cannot deceive the spirit within;   the
House of Sorrow is strange, all its furniture is
strange, and the newcomer must learn anew how
to live.

The first lesson is to accept the past as a beautiful day that is done, as the loveliness of a rose
that has withered away.   The object of our yearning has passed from the world of actual contacts
into the world of art.   Memory may paint the
picture as it will, drop out all shadows and catch
the beauty of our exquisite loss in all the golden
glow of human happiness.   There, within the
shrine prepared by Sorrow, that picture will ever
refresh us and bless us.   Evil cannot touch it, nor
ill-will, nor envy, nor sordid care;   only our own
faithlessness, our own acceptance of unworthy
things, can stain the freshness of its beauty.   Sorrow has constituted us the sacristans of this
shrine; on us rests the care of this pictured
relic, and, unless we suffer motes and beams
to get in our eyes, it will remain as bright in
the sanctuary of memory as in the sunshine of
earthly life.

The second lesson is to receive from Sorrow the gift that we have all asked for, begged for, a thousand times. We have felt the oppression of petty things, we have been caught in the nets of grossness, we have suffered ourselves to become captives and servants to the common and the mean, till, weary with servitude, we have cried out, "Oh, that I might rescue my soul!" And now the work of deliverance is accomplished and our souls are free. Tyranny has fallen from our necks. Vulgar inclinations have lost their ancient glamour, and the baser appetites shiver in their nakedness. Our wish has been granted; the prison doors are open wide, we may pursue with all our strength, with all the resolution we can summon, the things which we, when bound, believed that we longed for.

The third gift of Sorrow is that she will not suffer us to put up with artificial lights. We had been content with the candle-light of sensuous things, letting our souls float idly on the clouds of chance experience; we had accepted life as a voyage down a magic river of random happenings, satisfied with such beacons as guarded our temporal prosperity. But Sorrow, with one sweep of her hand, has extinguished all those lights, and robbed the things of sense of all their shimmering.

Sorrow has shown us that we live in the dark; and no great harm has been done, for we no longer care to see the flickering lights that once flared about our heads with so deceptive a glow. Sorrow has given us a yearning for inextinguishable light. All is dark; but all darkness is one great supplication for light which cannot be quenched. Shadow, mystery, blackness, the outer and the inner courts of chaos, all echo Sorrow's cry for light.

So the soul into which the iron has entered, amazed and offended by the bitterness of agony, turns to find some light, some principle, whose shining shall illume for her these random happenings of joy and sorrow which make up what we call life, whose wisdom shall satisfy her passionate demand for some explanation why she should have been conjured up out of nothingness, to be caressed and flattered for a season, and then stabbed to the heart. What is this universe that treats us so? What animates it? What is it trying to do? What is its attitude toward man?

Who shall explain these things? We have lost the support of the Christian dogmas, and we have no new staff to lean upon; we have strayed from the old road of hope, and we do not find a new road. What can science or philosophy do for us, — science that pays so little heed to the soul,

philosophy that pays so little heed to grief? We
must shift for ourselves and see what we can find.
Happiness left us content with happiness, but
Sorrow bids us rise up and seek something divine.

The first act must be to lift our eyes from
Sorrow, cast memory loose, put on the magic cap
of indifference and forgetfulness, and look out as
from a window upon the phenomena that may
chance to meet the eye, and see whether from the
sample we can infer a pattern, interwoven with a
thread of hope, for the whole fabric.

II

I look at the universe as it presents itself to me
this morning, as if I, for the first time, were making
its acquaintance. I find myself in a pleasant room.
Golden light, pouring in at the window, irradiates
shining breakfast things. A wonderful odour
greets my nostrils; a steaming fragrance, followed
by a delicious taste, quickens my whole being.
Next, round yellow fruit is presented to me,
smelling as if it remembered all its blossoming
origins or had packed its rind with ambrosia in
the garden of the Hesperides. Added to these is a
delicious bread, rich Rembrandtesque brown
without, ripe yellow within, a princely kind of
bread, which they tell me is called Johnny-cake.

Breakfast done, I walk out into an unroofed azure palace of light. Upon the ground a multitude of little green stalks intertwine with each other to keep my feet from touching the soil beneath; mighty giants, rooted to earth, hold up a hundred thousand leaves to shelter me from the excess of golden glory that illumines the azure palace; the leaves rustle, either for the music's sake or to let me feel their sentiment of kinship. Further on, little beautiful things, which have renounced locomotion, — recognizing that they have found their appointed places and are happy there, like the Lady Pia in the lower heaven of Paradise, — waft floral benedictions to me. And about them hover winged flowers that spread their petals to the breeze and flit from fragrance to fragrance. Into a honey-laden cornucopia, a passionate presence, its wings humming in wild ecstasy, dips its bill, while the sunlight burnishes the jewelled magnificence of its plumage.

A troop of young creatures, far more wonderful than these, passes by, with glancing eyes and rosy cheeks, making sweetest music of words and laughter. These, they tell me, are children, and they say that there are many of them, and that I, too, was once a child. I laugh at this preposterous flattery.

Another being, well-nigh ethereal, a naiad perhaps, or the imagining of some kindly god, trips by.
It is exquisite. The leaves cast their shadows
before it; the flowers tremble for pleasure.
"What is it?" I whisper. Some one answers
carelessly: "That is a maiden."

Then another young creature dances by, —
head erect, all animation, the breeze blowing its
hair back from what must be a temple for pure and
noble thought — like a gallant ship beating out
to sea. This, they tell me, is a youth.

I walk on and behold many goodly things. I
hear melodies that stir yearnings to which I can
give no name, start flashes of joy, or glimmering
understandings of the "deep and dazzling darkness" that surrounds the farthest reaches of terrestrial light. I am told that there are men,
called poets, who have built a palace out of their
crystal imaginations, where life and its doings are
depicted in a thousand ways, sometimes as in a
mirror, trait for trait, sometimes glorified, and all
in varied cadences of music. And I am told that
the wonderful things which greet my senses — dry
land and its fruitfulness, ocean, air, clouds, stars,
and sky — are but an infinitesimal fragment of an
infinite whole, in which the curious mind may
travel for countless ages and never reach the end

of eager and throbbing questionings; that there is between me and it the most wonderful of all relations, the contact, real or imaginary, of my consciousness with the great stream of phenomena that passes before it, and that this relation is the source of never-ending intellectual pleasure.

But more than by all things else I am impressed by the sentiments between creatures of my kind, between mother and son, father and daughter, husband and wife, friend and friend, a wonderful mutual attraction which makes each yield his will to the other and rouses a double joy, — from securing for the other and from renouncing for one's self, — a half-mystical bond that holds two together as gravitation holds terrestrial things to the earth, so sweet, so strong, so delicate, that the imagination cannot rise beyond this human affection at its height.

Such is the fragment of the universe which presents itself at this moment to my consciousness. Bewildered by wonders heaped on wonders, I cry out triumphantly, "Is there not evidence of friendliness to man here?"

III

But men of science answer, No. The cause or causes behind all that exists, they say, are neither friendly nor unfriendly; they are unconscious, indifferent, inexorable; they act willy nilly. They are blind forces. The attitude that man must hold toward them is an attitude neither of reverence nor worship; he must be wary, ever on his guard, and quick with intellectual curiosity. And Science gives names and more names to every movement, to every aspect, of the manifestations of force. And then when Science has defined and enumerated, and redefined and reënumerated to its heart's content, it expects us to look up in wonder and be grateful, as if names and definitions brought with them health and happiness. We do wonder, but we can feel no gratitude. We follow, as best we can, the teachings of Science. We acknowledge our incompetence, our ignorance, our inability to appreciate what we are taught. But to us an enumeration of processes and stages does not seem to be an explanation; that enumeration sounds as hollow to us as if science were to explain our personal existences by recounting every step our feet have taken since we first set foot to floor. Moreover, men of science bewilder us by their respect, pushed almost to obsequiousness, for bigness and littleness, for nearness and distance, for chemical energy and physical restlessness. Why should consciousness hold its breath before the very great or the very little, why should it duck and bend before unconscious energy ?   And where is the explanation or understanding of our two worlds, more real to us than ponderable matter or restless energy, our world of happiness and our world of sorrow ?

We turn for enlightenment to the Spirit of Life; but the Spirit of Life answers:

"My concern is with life, not with knowledge."

"Whom, then, shall we ask ?"

"Ask Pain and ask Love," replies the Spirit of Life.

Like little Jack Horner, science pulls out its plums, — electricity, radium, the chemical union of elements, the multiplication of cells, — and, like Jack, congratulates itself.   But to the inmates of the House of Sorrow, far more wonderful than all these things, far more mysterious, and demanding subtler thought, is human affection. For a generation past, human affection has been treated, and for years to come may still be treated, as the superfluous product of physico-chemical energies.   The scientific mind, elated by its victories, bivouacs on the old fields of battle.   But the real interest in atom and cell lies in the human consciousness, and the interest in consciousness lies in the human affections.   In themselves elec-

trons and cells are neither wonderful nor interesting; they are merely strange, and can claim only
the attention due to strangers. But human love
is of boundless interest to man, and should have the
pious devotion of the wisest and most learned men.

Science proceeds as if the past were the home
of explanation; whereas the future, and the future
alone, holds the key to the mysteries of the present.
When the first cell divided, the meaning of that
division was to be discovered in the future, not in
the past; when some prehuman ancestor first
uttered a human sound, the significance of that
sound was to be interpreted by human language,
not by apish grunts; when the first plant showed
solicitude for its seed, the interest of that solicitude lay in the promise of maternal affection.
Things must be judged in the light of the coming
morning, not of the setting stars.

It is not the past which, like an uncoiling spring,
pushes us on; creation faces the future, and is
drawn onward by an irresistible attraction. "For
though it be a maxim in the schools," says Thomas
Traherne, "*that there is no love of a thing unknown,*
yet I have found that things unknown have a
secret influence on the soul, and, like the centre of
the earth unseen, violently attract it. We love
we know not what. . . . As iron at a distance is

drawn by the loadstone, there being some invisible communications between them, so is there in us a world of love to somewhat, though we know not what. . . . There are invisible ways of conveyance by which some great thing doth touch our souls, and by which we tend to it. Do you not feel yourself drawn by the expectation and desire of some Great Thing?"

Life seems to have differentiated itself, developing a Promethean spirit within a grosser element. Life as a whole cares only to preserve itself, it seeks to live, it cringes and will accept existence on any terms, it will adapt itself to desert or dunghill; but the Promethean spirit seeks a higher and a higher sphere. This life within life — this *cor cordium* of existence — is surely travelling on a definite road. The very passion with which it takes its direction, its readiness to seize on pain and use to the full pain's ennobling properties, are our assurance that life follows an instinct within that guides it to that which is either its source or its full fruition. We must interpret the seed by the flower, not the flower by the seed. We must interpret life by its deepest attributes, by pain and by love.

Pain has been explained as an accompaniment of the Promethean spirit of life, which, in precipitate haste to proceed upon its journey, takes the most ready and efficacious path onward, heedless of what it breaks and crushes on the way. But pain is rather an impulse within the spirit of life. Pain is its conscience urging it on. Unless we were pricked on by pain, we should wish to stand still, content with our own satisfaction, meanly indifferent to higher pleasures; without pain all life might have been content to house itself in low animal forms, and wallow in bestiality, ease, and lust. It may be that the onward progress might have been accomplished without pain; we might have been whirled upward, insensible, toward the universal goal. But we have received the privilege of consciously sharing in the upward journey, so that each onward movement must be a wrench from the past, each moment a parting, each step an eternal farewell. These noble inconstancies are tasks imposed by pain.

In its humblest capacity pain serves as a danger signal for the body's health, or as punishment for precautions neglected; even here, however, it is more spiritual than corporeal, for it is the means by which the soul arouses the body to perpetual vigilance in the service of Life. Pain must concern itself with corporeal things, because consciousness is dependent upon the body; it must discharge its share of the general tribute that consciousness, as a dependency, pays to the body. But such services as pain may render in the material world cannot account for all pain; they cannot account for the heartache, for the depth and breadth of anguish, for the sombre majesty of grief. An explanation must be sought elsewhere.

Pain is a function of the soul; it fosters the preservation and spiritual growth of conscious life. The pangs of conscience, the agony of the heart, nourish the tenderer elements of consciousness; they root out the docks and darnels of worldly pleasure, and so protect the little nurslings of the spirit that would else have been choked, nursing them with passion and tears, as Nature nurses with sunshine and with rain.

No man can say by what means inorganic matter brought forth organic creation; nor can we say how the corporeal organism, seemingly content with processes of material decomposition and reintegration, generated mind. These great deeds were done in the dark, they have left no witnesses; but we have the testimony of our feelings that some momentous change, comparable to these great changes, is even now taking place, however slow its progress may be. Consciousness, in its own ideal world, is seething with independent

vitality, eager to develop itself, eager to give
birth to a more spiritual state, eager to help Life
take another great onward step.   The excesses of
pain, that serve no corporeal purpose, seem to be
caused by the violent efforts of the Spirit of Life
in its struggles to take such a step; but, in reality,
pain is the cause rather than the effect.

Charged, therefore, with such possibilities in
the service of Life, pain — its capacities little
taxed by duties of guardianship and nurture —
rises to nobler offices; it gradually becomes a
closer and closer companion to Life, it twines its
tendrils round the tree of Life, it grafts itself on
like a branch, and becomes incorporate with Life
itself, an essential element in vital energy, a function of some vital, spiritual organ.   Yet this organ is not yet established at a definite task, for
at times pain seems to be the trenchant edge of
the Life spirit, cutting and purging the soul from
whatever may impede her upward progress; at
times, in the soul's more tranquil moods, pain
seems to be a homesickness for the home that Life
aspires to create.   Moreover, pain partakes of
the vast variety of Life; it announces the prick
of a needle on the finger, or sweeps over the soul
in the beauty of tragedy with awe-inspiring flight.
Science, which deals with the things that are past,

unable to fit pain into utilitarian categories, repeats its vaso-motor formulas; but faith, which deals with things that are to be, hails it as the prophet of a new heaven and a new earth. What better explanation of pain is there than that it is the birth pangs of spirit, the assurance of new things unseen?

In this work of lifting life to a higher stage, pain is but one of many ministers, the most terrible, the most efficient. All the forces of life work to that end. The struggle for life, often ascribed to the egotism of the individual, is not properly so ascribed. That struggle is undertaken in obedience to the law of upward progress. Each vegetable and animal is in honor bound to carry on its individual life to the uttermost, for who can tell before the event what road Life will take upon its upward journey. Each is bound to make itself a path for Life to take. The acorn, the seed of the dandelion, the spawn of the herring, the man-child, must hold themselves always ready to carry Life upon the next onward stage; each claims the honor for itself and chooses to kill and to risk death rather than forego the chance of such supreme dignity. In the struggle for self-preservation lies the fulfilment of the creature's allegiance to life. The struggle for life means pain

inflicted and pain received; but in pain lies the
honor of the organic world. We cannot imagine
nobility or dignity without pain. Lower things
do not experience it. Common men always flee
from it and execrate it; but, now and then, here
and there, men and women seek it out. They
may quiver in agony, they may succumb momen-
tarily to the weakness of the flesh, but they bear
witness that pain is good. For them pain is the
ploughing and harrowing which must precede
seed-time and harvest. These men we have
been taught to call saints and heroes. Shall we
give no weight to their testimony?

IV

As it is with pain, so is it with human love.
Each is a turning toward the light ahead. The
mutual attraction of cells has no meaning till it
appears as the first effort of nature on her way to
produce human affection. At every stage in the
drawing together of cells and multiples of cells,
whether in polyp, reptile, or ape, the significance
of that drawing together lies in that for which
it is preparing the way. So, too, is it with human
affections: they shine with a light not their own,
but reflected from the higher significance of the
future. Our love is but a pale anticipation of that

K

love which the universe is striving to round out to full-orbed completeness. Love, at least, offers an explanation of the goal of life, — life struggling to consciousness, consciousness rising to love. All other things find their explanation in something higher, but love is its own fulfilment.

Love has no doubts. To itself love is the very substance of reality. The phenomena of sight, sound, touch, and their fellows, are but the conditions under which life has made a foothold for itself in this boisterous world; the senses know nothing beyond their own functioning, they have nothing to say regarding the end or purpose of life. But to love, — all the labor and effort of all the universe, with all its sidereal systems, with all its ethereal immensity, has been for the sake of producing love. Of what consequence is it, whether insensible matter endure a myriad years, or assume infinite bigness? In the absence of consciousness, an infinity of matter is as nothing. One flash of conscious life illumined by love is worth all the patience, all the effort, all the labor, of unconscious energy throughout an infinity of time. Consciousness is but a minister to love, to the love that is to be.

Science, with its predilection for sensuous things, for enumerations, classifications, explanations, in terms of matter and energy, asserts that consciousness fulfils no useful function at all. Consciousness is an accidental creation, shot out like a random spark by the friction of living, a sort of tramp that has stolen a ride on the way. According to this theory the musician would continue to play his fiddle whether he produced a melody or not; the endless chain of propulsions from behind would impel one hand to finger the strings, the other to ply the bow. But to the non-scientific man, consciousness is the achievement to which the universe has bent all its energies.

Had the universe taken a different turn, or had it neglected the things which it has done, consciousness as we know it would never have come into being. But consciousness has come, and the assertion that it is a superfluous thing, an accident, seems to have been hatched from the very wilfulness of arrogance. Because science — a virtuoso in motion, in attractions and repulsions — has not yet discovered the function of consciousness, is it not premature to say that consciousness has no function? To the common mind the obvious function of consciousness — in addition to the minor occupations which its genesis from matter has imposed upon it — is to experience love, and thereby give a reasonable meaning to the universe.

If matter, or energy, has succeeded in creating consciousness, even though only on our planet and in such little measure, may it not be that after other æons of restless activity, consciousness in its turn shall generate another state of being to which science (then absorbed by a predilection for consciousness, as it is now absorbed by its predilection for sensuous things) will deny any useful function, but which shall justify itself as consciousness does to-day? May it not be — if we let ourselves listen to the incantations of hope — that this higher spiritual sensitiveness, generated by consciousness, will create as much difference between the new order of creatures that shall possess it and ourselves, as there is now between us and inorganic matter? Does not the experience of those men who — in daily life scarce realizing material things — have felt themselves rapt into the presence of God, point to some such inference? "When love has carried us above all things . . . we receive in peace the Incomprehensible Light, enfolding us and penetrating us." But whatever our laboring, sweating universe may bring forth, this seems to be the direction it has taken, the goal that it has set before itself.

Is it not odd that men should continue to interpret love in terms of the atom and the cell, of chemistry and physics, when the whole significance of all the doings of matter and energy comes from our human consciousness?

But shall they that suffer pain to-day, that have once lived in the Eden of love, shall these enter into the light of the day that is to dawn?

Epilogue

The traveller sighed, lost in perplexity; and the Spirit of Life said, "Come, let us walk in the courts of the House of Sorrow." So they walked through the courts, and the newcomer beheld in the House a great multitude of windows, most of which were dark, as if there was no light within, or, as if the curtains were drawn and the shutters closed. But other windows shot forth rays of light, some faint and feeble, some stronger, while others poured forth a flood of brightness.

"Why are some of the windows so bright?" inquired the newcomer; and the Spirit of Life answered, "Those are the windows of the light-bearers; their inmates display lights, some more, some less."

"With what do they feed their lights?" asked the newcomer.

"A few shine of their own nature," answered the Spirit, "as if they drew upon an inexhaustible source within; but most of them burn the oil of hope."

"If they have no hope, what then?" asked the newcomer.

"Then," said the Spirit, "they must make their light from pain. There is an old saying, 'He that doth not burn, shall not give forth light.' The past lightened you with its brightness; but by your own shining you must lighten the present and the future. Hope gives the readier light; but even if hope fail, none need leave their windows dark, for where you have pain at your disposal, unlimited pain, it should not require great spiritual ingenuity to use that pain for fuel."

The newcomer bowed his head, and the Spirit of Life led him to his appointed room within the house.

A FORSAKEN GOD

I

AN Englishman of letters who, in the eyes of Americans at least, embodies the spirit of Oxford and Cambridge, expressed not long ago certain frank opinions about America. What motive induced him to tell the world what he thinks of us? It could not have been mere excitement over novel experiences. Englishmen of letters no longer write about America in the spirit of explorers. Mr. Lowes Dickinson could hardly have appeared to himself — reflected in the delicate mirror of his mind — as a gentleman adventurer, staring from a peak of Greek culture at our amazing characteristics, and differing from stout Cortez mainly in not being silent. The war had not yet begun; there was no motive for bringing gentle suasion — such as may be implied in any expression of British interest in America — to bear upon our neutrality. The readiest explanation of his writing is that he was prompted by a simple motive: he wrote under the need of saying what was on his mind. This is the very kind of criticism to give ear to. When the human heart must unburden itself of a load, it neither flatters nor detracts; it acts instinctively with no thought of consequences. The mood is a mood of truth. The man who speaks the truth to us is our best friend, and we should always listen to him.

Among other things Mr. Dickinson said, "Describe the average Western man and you describe the American; from east to west, from north to south, everywhere and always the same — masterful, aggressive, unscrupulous, egotistic, and at once good-natured and brutal, kind if you do not cross him, ruthless if you do, greedy, ambitious, self-reliant, active for the sake of activity, intelligent and unintellectual, quick-witted and crass, contemptuous of ideas but amorous of devices, valuing nothing but success, recognizing nothing but the actual. . . .

"The impression America makes on me is that the windows are blocked up. It has become incredible that this continent was colonized by the Pilgrim Fathers. . . . Religion is becoming a department of practical business. The churches — orthodox and unorthodox, old and new, Christian, Christian-Scientific, theosophic, higher-thinking — vie with one another in advertising goods which are all material benefits:

'Follow me, and you will get rich,' 'Follow me, and you will get well,' 'Follow me, and you will be cheerful, prosperous, successful.' Religion in America is nothing if not practical."

Some Americans do not like this criticism. They protest that the critic has no eye for the essential qualities which render our country dear to us, that he gazes dimly, through a mist of Cambridge traditions, from some spleen-producing point of vision, upon a people spiritually remote from him. Human nature instinctively lays flattering unction to its soul; but there is only one right way to take the fault-finding of an intellectual and highly educated man, and that is to see how much truth there is in his fault-finding and then strive to correct our faults. Most Americans do not care about the opinions of Oxford and Cambridge; they say that we must be a law unto ourselves, and absorb nourishment from the sunshine of our own self-esteem. But others, less robust, do set store by the opinion of scholars bred, for the greater part, upon the recorded mind of the most gifted people that has ever lived in Europe, — upon the books of Homer and Pindar, Æschylus and Euripides, Plato and Aristotle, and their fellows. It will do us less harm to assume that there is too much truth in what Mr. Dickinson has said of us, than to assume that there is none.

II

Sixty or seventy years ago, a definite conception of the moral and intellectual mould upon which men should shape themselves, appeared to be solidly established. That conception was definite and readily accepted because it actually had been embodied in a living man, Johann Wolfgang von Goethe. Emerson, Lowell, Bayard Taylor, each in his respective way, and all other leaders of thought in America, acknowledged Goethe as the model for man, as an intellectual being, to strive to imitate.

Goethe's position seemed as secure as Shakspere's, Dante's, or Homer's. Lower than they in the supreme heights of song, he was more universal. He had composed poetry that in peculiar sweetness rivalled the Elizabethan lyrics and surpassed them in variety and depth of thought; he had written a play judged equal to *Hamlet* or the Book of Job; he had written romances that rivalled *I Promessi Sposi* in nice depiction of the soul's workings, and were as interesting in their delineation of human life as the most romantic of the Waverley Novels. He had been the chief

counsellor of a sovereign prince, and had devised
wise policy in a hundred matters of statecraft.
His mind had put forth ideas as a tree in spring-
time puts forth leaves; his speculations had
travelled in wide fields of scientific thought; he
had divined certain processes concerning the
origin of species in a manner that still associates
his name with the names of Lamarck and Darwin.
He was accoutred with a radiant intelligence, with
unmatched cultivation, with wide sympathies; he
was free from prejudice to a degree unequalled
in our modern world. His intellectual impartiality
had inspired a sect of persons with the creed that
the home of man is the free mind, and that his country is coterminous with the whole range of truth.

Great as were his feats in literature and in
science, his special achievement was the creation
of his ideal for the living of life, an ideal that
seemed founded on so broad a base that it could
but be a question of time and perception for it to
be universally acknowledged and adopted. More
than any man, from Aristotle to Thomas Aquinas,
from Aquinas to Auguste Comte, he seemed to
have a true view of the ideal proper for the human
spirit.

Goethe's ideal embraces freedom from the
prejudices of home and education, clearness of

vision, courage in the teeth of circumstance, an ordered life, a disciplined spirit, an unclouded soul, the pursuit of knowledge for the sake of knowledge, and the disinterested worship of whatever is perfect.

Nobility, order, measure, and the underlying feeling of peace, are primary elements in Goethe's ideal. These qualities, if there be any remedy anywhere, make the antidote to the evils which, according to Mr. Lowes Dickinson, beset us. They exalt the things of the intellect, and take away temptation to the "unscrupulous," "brutal" pursuit of material things. And more medicinal than all the others is Goethe's belief in inward peace. Under the impulsion of instinct, we Americans move to and fro, go up and down, and turn about. We seek satisfaction for our appetites in activity. Goethe lived in the world and was of the world, and yet he sought peace of soul. He sought peace, not to escape from the world, but to gain greater dominion over it. He hoped to obtain greater control over the happenings of life, — greater power to put them to use and to enjoyment, — by penetrating into the deeps of serenity; he desired mastery over self as a means to inward peace, and inward peace as a means to mastery over life.

We have drifted so far from the opinions of
Emerson and his contemporaries, and — if Mr.
Dickinson is right in his criticisms — we have so
completely lost sight of the example set by Goethe,
that I will expatiate a little upon what Goethe was,
and might still be to us.

III

For Goethe, inward peace was not the final
goal, but a stage on the way; or, rather, it was
the sustenance of life, the means of right living,
the power that should help him become himself,
help him grow to his full stature. And the problem of his self-education was how to attain this
inward peace. For him, as for all seekers in the
Christian past, the conventional way would have
been to follow Christian teachings; and there is
evidence that Christian teachings touched him,
touched him deeply. They stirred him somewhat
as Gothic architecture stirred his enthusiasm in
youth. But the whole trend of his nature pre-
vented this. To Goethe the mediæval search-
ings after God were dead hypotheses; the road
that led Richard of St. Victor or St. Francis of
Assisi to peace, was to him a blind alley. Goethe
did not wish to escape from the world, from its
perturbations and disquiet. He desired inward

peace, as a hero, resolute to fight and conquer, might wish for a shield.

Another path was to follow the precepts of the pagan philosophers, such counsels as the imperial spokesman of ancient Stoicism gives : "Men seek retreats for themselves, houses in the country, seashores, and mountains; but this is altogether a mark of the most common sort of men, for it is in a man's power, whenever he shall choose, to retire into himself. For nowhere either with more quiet or more freedom from trouble does a man retire than into his own soul, particularly when he has within him such thoughts that by looking into them he is immediately in perfect tranquillity; and I affirm that tranquillity is nothing else than the good ordering of the mind."

The Stoics wished to retire into their own souls in order that they might come back to the world free from discontent with worldly things; whereas, Goethe wished to come back into the world with power to dominate worldly things. He was therefore obliged to devise a path for himself, a path far nearer to the pagan than to the Christian path, but still a new path. Might not a devout man, one who believed that "*Das Schaudern ist der Menschheit bestes Teil*," — that "the tremulous sense of awe is man's noblest attribute," —

attain peace by way of the intellect, by living life
in noble completeness? The affirmative answer
was the essential thesis of Goethe's life. He
maintained this not so much by what he wrote, as
by his conduct. He was no disciple of the mystics; he did not propose to overcome this life of
phenomena by passing beyond phenomena, but
by comprehending them. He never aspired to
spread his wings and fly to Heaven; he kept his
feet planted on solid earth. Madame de Staël
says: "*Goethe ne perd jamais terre, tout en atteig-
nant aux conceptions les plus sublimes*" — "Goethe
never quits the earth, even when reaching up to
the most sublime ideas." And yet his firm stand
upon earth and his concern with things of this
world did not tempt him to adopt worldly meas-
ures. "*On diroit qu'il n'est pas atteint par la vie*"
— "the things of this world do not seem to touch
him." These qualities of his that Madame de
Staël noted are signs that the seeker had attained.
All, or almost all, testimony concerning Goethe's
presence, his manner, his dignity, is in accord.
To Eckermann, who did not see him till he was an
old man, he seemed "*wie einer, der von himm-
lischem Frieden ganz erfüllt ist*" — "like a man
brimful of heavenly peace." All his life he
sought knowledge, for, as he believed, knowledge

begets understanding, and understanding sympathy, and sympathy brings the spirit into harmony with all things, and harmony engenders peace. Goethe is the great embodiment of the return of the modern mind to the religion of the classic spirit, seeking inward peace, not in an unseen heaven, but in "the good ordering of the mind."

Goethe's seeking was not the seeking of a man of letters; it was not prompted by the artist's instinct, not consciously adopted as a means to master his art; it was the seeking of the human spirit for the road to salvation on earth. Take the long series of his works, — poems, plays, novels, criticisms; they reveal no obsessing preoccupation with the attainment of a high serenity of soul. They represent the adventures of his spirit with the multitudinous happenings of human life. But here and there, like light through a chink, flashes out evidence of the direction in which his soul is set.

Nevertheless, the dominance of the idea of inward peace is far more apparent from the story of his life than from his writings. Peace shaped itself in his mind not as a Nirvana, not as a rapt contemplation of God, but as harmony, as a state of inward unity, of a right relation to the universe, manifest to men as order, proportion, measure, serenity, and therefore, necessarily, in relation to other men, as benevolence. In this he was powerfully helped by the strong intellectual influence that swept over Germany in his youth, the admiration for classical art taught by Winckelmann and Lessing. Under the teachings of these two men, the stately grandeur of classical sculpture and architecture appeared to be the summit of human attainment, the goal of imitation and effort. He learned that "*Das Ideal der Schönheit ist Einfalt und Stille*" — "the ideal of beauty is simplicity and repose."

The theories of Winckelmann and of Lessing fermented in Goethe's mind, and, when he came to make his famous *Italienische Reise*, they fairly seethed and boiled. The beauty of repose became his sole idea of beauty. His admiration of the Ludovisi Juno, he says, was his first love affair in Italy. At Vicenza he stopped in admiration before the Palladian palaces. "When we stand face to face with these buildings, then we first realize their great excellence; their bulk and massiveness fill the eye, while the lovely harmony of their proportions, admirable in the advance and recession of perspective, brings peace to the spirit." When he went to Assisi, he gave a wide berth to the Basilica of St. Francis, half appre-

L

hensive lest its Gothic elements might bring confusion into his thoughts, walked straight to the
Temple of Minerva, and enjoyed "a spectacle
that bestowed peace on both eye and mind."
Deep in his nature, this preoccupation with what
shall bring peace is hard at work.

At bottom Goethe preferred art to life; he preferred to see the doings and passions of men
reflected in the artist's mirror rather than to see
them in the actual stuff of existence. Naturally,
the prevalent notion concerning the classical
world as a world of harmony, of calm, of self-
control, found his spirit most sympathetic. At
the age of forty, on the return from his Italian
travels, he accepted the great pagan tradition in
the form that Marcus Aurelius left it: "It is in
thy power to live free from all compulsion in the
greatest tranquillity of mind. . . . I affirm that
tranquillity is nothing else than the good ordering
of the mind." That to Goethe is the gist of all
right thinking about life, and he spent his own
long life in the effort to express it in his behaviour.

Goethe's idea of harmony, of beauty, of measure, of right relations with the universe, was, of
course, not a mere pagan ideal in the sense which
we usually give to the word pagan; it was essen-
tially a religious conception, — religious rather in

the Hellenic than in the Hebraic sense, for the
pagan element, with its tinge of pride in dominat-
ing the untoward in life, is always there. In early
life his religious sentiments were profoundly
affected by the evangelical traditions of Protestant
Germany, which saturated the atmosphere of
Frankfort; afterwards they wore a more philosophical hue, but they were always strong enough
to counteract the pagan inclination of his mind to
rest content at the stage of peace attainable by
knowledge and self-control. The problem before
him was how to reconcile the transcendental impulses of his spirit with the ideal of a harmonious
whole. For the most part, his anti-ecclesiastical
conception of freedom, and the pagan training of
his mind, turned him away from current Christianity; he treated it as he treated the Basilica
of St. Francis at Assisi, he simply did not go out
of his way to look at it. He took much from
Spinoza. The potential divinity within him inspired him with reverence. He desired to gain
the composure and elevation of soul becoming to
a man who is animated by the divine spirit that
permeates all nature. From Italy he wrote, "I
should like to win eternity for my spirit." And
after his return, he grew steadily more sensitive
to the deep current that propels the soul toward

the unknown. Gradually he approached, by his own way, the borders of that spiritual region in which Plato puts the soul. Later he hid his face in thick clouds of symbolism; but his mystical inclination — *die Erhebung ins Unendliche* — never dominated his notion of a complete human being with moral and intellectual nature fashioned on a heroic model, fit, as it were, to be lodged in a body carved by Skopas. He reached the point where he united harmoniously the sense of measure, of beauty, of peace through knowledge, with a tremulous sensitiveness to the possibilities that tenant the vast unknown which surrounds our little kingdom of sense.

To set forth such an ideal as this to the world was Goethe's self-appointed task. No other man, perhaps, in the whole history of the civilized world, has been so well fitted by nature and education for such a feat. Dante, a greater poet and a greater man, was too emotional, too passionate, ever to care to hold up what to him would have been the intolerable composure of the Stoic spirit. Cervantes, notwithstanding his clear-eyed compassion and his high reverence for the spiritual light in the human soul, was far too lacking in general culture, even to essay the task. Milton was too partisan, too dogmatic; Shakspere too

averse to any idea of teaching men in any way
other than by letting his sunshine play on human
life. And, in our own day, Tolstoï became too
blind to classical beauty and to harmony of the
soul, too devoted to traditional Christian ideas,
to be capable of any such endeavor.

Goethe's calm spirit, his loyalty to fact, his
habit "of standing on the solid earth," his practice, as he says, "*Alle Dinge wie sie sind zu sehen*,"
—" to see all things as they are," — were to men
of a rational way of thinking a guarantee that he
would not, upon Dædalian wings, essay a flight
of folly and destruction; and his sensitiveness to
those vague reactions and movings that stir in
the deeps of the human spirit assured men with
mystical yearnings that he was not cut off from
their fellowship. For him, as well as for them,
there is a region — whether it be in man's soul
here and now, or elsewhere — where

> Alles Vergängliche
> Ist nur ein Gleichniss;
> Das Unzulängliche
> Hier wird's Ereigniss.

Or, as Bayard Taylor translates it:

> All things transitory
> But as symbols are sent;
> Earth's insufficiency
> Here grows to Event.

IV

Here, then, was an ideal which, one would think, should have been a shining light to our world to-day, — the classic spirit embodied in man's life, manifesting beauty, harmony, measure, self-restraint, accompanied by an open-eyed, unprejudiced outlook on all things old and new, and with all the windows which look toward things divine uncurtained and unshuttered. Why has it fallen?

It may be said that modern life is opposed to such an ideal as Goethe's; and it may be — as Mr. Dickinson probably thinks — that American nature is too friable a material to endure the carving of Hellenic souls. But, be that as it may, it is apparent that the failure to follow Goethe's ideal is a universal failure, almost as pitiful in Europe as with us; and the answer to the question, why has this ideal fallen, must be sought in causes that operate in Europe as well as in America.

One can see plainly several forces, good and bad, at work, — among them, science, luxury, the national spirit, the humanitarian movement, and democracy.

Science has drawn into its service a large part of the nobler spirits among men, and inspired them with the narrower doctrine of seeking out the ways of nature. But science, if it has diverted many men who might have followed Goethe's Hellenic idealism, has in many ways supported his views: it serves truth, if not the whole truth, it encourages in its servitors simplicity of life, it places their rewards largely in the satisfaction of the spirit. On the other hand, modern science tends to overvalue the inanimate at the expense of life; it encourages the notion that final truth may be weighed, measured, and tested; too often it lays stress on knowledge for utility's sake, rather than for the sake of knowledge itself, or, as Goethe would have done, for the increase of sympathy which knowledge brings. By directing attention to the manifold phenomena outside the real self — to heavenly bodies, to the substances of our planet, to plants, germs, fossils, atoms, electrons, and all the phenomena of the sensible universe — and to our minds and bodies as things apart from ourselves, it necessarily belittles the importance of the rounded perfection of self, the importance of equilibrium in the sum of a man's relations to all things that are and to all things that may be.

Science always concentrates attention on one small portion of life. There is no science of life as a whole; none that teaches us our relations to the universe. Science in itself is an unreal thing, an abstraction; we no longer have science, but sciences. Like the children of. Saturn, they have destroyed their father. There are physics, chemistry, botany, astronomy, geology, palæontology, zoölogy, psychology, and many others, all destined to be divided and subdivided, and there will be as many more as there are objects of intellectual curiosity in the universe. The swing of scientific thought is centripetal; each science is a jealous god and will have no other gods share in its worship. The field of attention for each servant of science grows smaller and smaller. It would be as impossible now for a man to be a great poet and a great man of science, like Goethe, as for a man to be familiar with the whole sum of contemporary knowledge, as Dante was. Devotion to science, in this century, is necessarily followed by some such experience as that which Darwin underwent; the meticulous observation of facts blunts all finer sensitiveness to poetry and music. Science means specialization, and dwells on the multiplicity of phenomena; Goethe wished a universal outlook, and was preoccupied with that unity which binds all to all.

Luxury, the application of man's control over

the forces of nature to self-indulgence, sets the
centre of gravity for human life in material things.
Luxury is the care of our brother, the body, —
St. Francis used to call it Brother Ass, — care so
assiduous, so elaborated, so refined, that it ap-
proaches to worship, and necessarily crowds out
the care and solicitude that should be devoted to
the soul. "Painting the outward walls so costly
gay" is a far easier art, much more within reach
of the successful many, than the decoration of the
soul. The organization of modern industry, the
multiplication of machinery, by giving more and
more to those who have already, strengthens the
thews and muscles of luxury. Luxury is head-
strong, potent in its dominion over fashion, unscrupulous in imposing its customs and opinions,
insolent in trampling down all in its way. This
is what is meant by the phrase "a materialistic
age"; it is the substitution of an easy art for a
difficult art, of a gross material, the body, which
demands the attention of the gymnast, the masseur,
the chiropodist, for a fine material, the soul, which
demands the service of the intellect and of the
spirit. There is no danger that our Brother the
Body will ever be neglected, or that material
things will be despised. Goethe was no disciple
of our Lady Poverty; but he held that a man's

wealth consists less in what he owns than in what he thinks and in what he is.

National sentiment has had a mighty career in the nineteenth century, witness Italy, Germany, Greece, Bulgaria, Servia, as well as the United States; and has by no means confined itself to political patriotism, witness the attempted revival of the Irish language and of Provençal; but whether patriotism concern a race, a nation, a language, or a cult, it is by its very definition a limitation. The Preacher of universal compassion said, "Whosoever shall do the will of my Father which is in Heaven, the same is my brother and sister and mother." Patriotism has its own virtues, but among them is not that of maintaining Goethe's ideals. Even during Germany's war of liberation against Napoleon, Goethe was absolutely indifferent to patriotism, at least in its political form. He maintained the position

> Da wo wir lieben
> Ist's Vaterland —

(there where we love is our country).

Then there is the strong current of humanitarianism, which tends to regard man as an animal with material wants, and spends itself on factory legislation, hygiene, sanitation, and almsgiving.

Goethe was not deficient in benevolence toward
his fellow men; but he subordinated this interest
to his prime concern for completeness, for mould-
ing within the individual a harmonious, beautiful,
heroic nature; and since such an ideal for the
mass of men is outside the pale of achievement,
he did not extend his serious interest to them.

V

Added to these — and this cause of the failure
of Goethe's ideals has perhaps been more effective
in America than elsewhere — stands democracy
and all democracy means. Democracy has solid
foundations of its own, — just as patriotism, humanitarianism, and science have, — and possesses
its own defenders and eulogists. Goethe was not
among them. He was an aristocrat; he believed
in the government of the best in all departments
of human society. The right of the best to dominate, even at the expense of the inferior, was to
him axiomatic. Democracy, with its tenderness
toward the incompetent multitude, with its ideas
of equality and fraternity, with its indifference to
quality when quantity is concerned, with its
good-humored inefficiency and its vulgar self-
satisfactions, was wholly alien to his spirit. He
felt no equality or fraternity between himself and

the multitude. In democracy the mass of the people possess not merely a voice in the political government, but also a voice in the moral government of the nation, a share in the formation of the ethical, intellectual, sentimental, and ideal character of the people. Goethe would as soon have trusted these supreme interests to Demos, as Don Quixote would have intrusted his knightly honor to Sancho's keeping. Goethe regarded man primarily as a creature charged with the duty, and endowed with the possibility, of self-perfectioning; but democracy values men according as they possess distinct and special capacities, according as they can do the immediate task needful to be done. Democracy, having many interests of its own, pays little or no heed to matters not congenial to it. Democracy is indifferent to form, because for democracy form and substance have no necessary relation; but to Goethe form and substance were one. Democracy is indifferent to elegance, because elegance is unsuitable to the multitude. Democracy cares little for beauty, because beauty establishes a caste apart.

Democracy neglects art, for art rests upon the privileges of nature, upon the endowment of gifted individuals, upon special sensitiveness and special capacities; art, by its very nature, means achievement by the few, enjoyment by the few. Democracy looks to the achievements and the enjoyments of the many. Aristocracy is the assertion of quality, of rareness of vision, of clearness of conception, of refinement and finish; it lays stress on the unusual, on the beneficent injustice of nature that enables lesser men to have greater men to look up to, and charges the greater men with deep personal responsibility. Democracy tends to belittle reverence, for reverence is devotion to that which is greater than ourselves, and seeks to find an object on which to spend itself. The reverent soul must believe in something greater than itself, whether in the human or the superhuman; it discovers, it unfolds, and, if necessary, imagines, something above itself. But Democracy has a passion for levelling, for reducing all to a common plane, so that no one shall complain that others have more than he, or are better placed. Such, at least, are some of the criticisms which the few pass upon the ideals of the many.

It is the same with the democratic idea of fraternity. What, aristocracy asks, is the worth of brotherhood unless brothers have a goodly heritage to divide? The important thing is to create an inheritance, whether of beauty, of

virtue, of glory; then let who can possess it.
The two points of view also take issue over the
idea of liberty. Democracy too easily abases its
conception of liberty to the liberty to eat and
sleep, the liberty to lie back and fold one's arms,
the liberty to be active for activity's sake (as Mr.
Dickinson says of us), liberty to do what to one's
self seems good; whereas aristocracy demands
self-renunciation for the sake of an ideal, demands
discipline, obedience, sacrifice. Democracy tends
to set a high value on comfort, on freedom from
danger, on "joy in commonalty spread"; whereas
aristocracy asserts the necessity of danger and of
pain in the education of man. Democracy values
human quantity, aristocracy human quality.
Democracy tends to render the intellect subser-
vient to the emotions, while aristocracy tends to
put emotion to the service of the intellect.

There are good grounds upon which democracy
may be eulogized, — the ground of justice, for
example; that was not Mr. Dickinson's business
nor is it mine; democracy's main fault consists
in its failure to confine itself to economic matters,
to politics, to material things, — consists in over-
flowing its proper limits and touching matters
with which it has no proper concern. Goethe
had little sympathy with democracy, especially

in the violent form which it assumed in his day,
in those manifestations that accompanied and
followed the French Revolution.

Another influence, springing from science, humanitarianism, and democracy, adds its strength
to theirs. Goethe's ideal for the human spirit,
however different from the ideals of democracy,
bears no small analogy to the Christian's ideal of
the soul. For the Christian the soul is everything, life is its opportunity, pleasure is a means
of acquiring strength by renunciation, grief an
aid to mounting higher, earthly losses are spiritual
gains; his highest hope is to render his soul as
perfect, as beautiful, as fully in accord with celestial harmonies, as may be. In Goethe this ideal
was replaced by the ideal of a human spirit that
triumphs over the obstacles of life, uses the affections, the passions even, for fuller self-develop-
ment; that aims at the harmonious fulfilment
of all its capacities, and seeks knowledge for the
sake of finer communion with deity in nature.
The trend of practical religion, under the pressure
of humanitarianism, is to regard the devotion that
strives to render the soul perfect, as a form of
egotism, and a kindred feeling swells the general
flood of modern conceptions that have swept away
Goethe's ideals.

It might have been thought that the religious element in Goethe's ideal would have saved it in America, if anywhere, from destruction; for we are a religious, or at least, as Mr. Dickinson would say, a superstitious people. Goethe's sympathetic approval of the theory that the human spirit tends toward a point of gravity at the centre of our universe, is consonant with permanent human needs; so is his sense of form, of beauty, of dignity. But whether it be the effect of democracy, of a childlike desire for novelty, of an undisciplined impatience with tradition, or of self-confidence in our power to create new forms of religion that shall more fully satisfy our own needs, or whatever the cause, the reasonableness, the conservatism, the restraint that mark the religious element in Goethe's ideal, have accomplished nothing to maintain that ideal with us.

So far it would appear that the causes which have combined to overthrow Goethe's ideals are scarcely more American than European; and that theory is confirmed by the popular attitude toward Goethe's ideals in Germany, where they seem to have fared no better than elsewhere. The old gods of serenity and beauty, Goethe and Beethoven, have been taken down from their pedestals, and Bismarck and Wagner have been

set up in their stead. The ideal of duty toward
self has certainly not suffered loss of power, but
the self that is the object of duty is a self of
dominion, not over fate and inward lack of harmony, but of dominion over other men. The
heroic model is no longer that of Phœbus Apollo,
but of a sinewed and muscular Thor. Domination, not harmony, is the teaching of the most
eminent German of letters since Schopenhauer. It
is true that Nietzsche is the greatest upholder of
aristocracy since Goethe; but Nietzsche did not
care for measure, proportion, harmony, pure
beauty. The whole development of Germany, —
the most brilliant there has been since that of
Italy of the Renaissance, — in energy, in material
well-being, in orderliness, in science, in self-
confidence, in ambition, has moved far from the
conception of full-minded completeness of character, intellect, and spirit, which Goethe taught
in confidence that, like light in the dark, like
warmth in the cold, such completeness would
receive the gratitude and honor of men.

Are we not forced to the conclusion that the
Zeitgeist is opposed to Goethe's ideals, that Mr.
Dickinson's criticism fits democracy and its
attendant phenomena rather than America? Is
it not democracy rather than America that is

M

"contemptuous of ideas, but amorous of devices"?
The Latin democratic countries must be excepted,
for Latins have a natural gift for form and a
special respect for intellectual accomplishment
that colors even their democracy; besides, democracy comes to them more naturally than to
northern peoples.   But if Mr. Dickinson had been
travelling in Australia, New Zealand, or Canada,
would he not have come to very much the same
conclusion?

Our neglect to follow Goethe's ideal, however,
remains our own fault, even if other democratic
countries have committed the same fault.   We
have brought Mr. Dickinson's criticism on our
own heads.   We must profit by that criticism,
and return to Goethe's ideal.   Some steps to be
taken are obvious.   First of all we must fully
satisfy the democratic desires of the *Zeitgeist* by
making the spirit of pure democracy prevail in all
matters of politics and economics, either by giving pure democracy supreme power over these
matters, or, supposing that there is some other
way to accomplish the same result, then by giving supreme power to the forces that can put
such other way into effect.   Then, when democracy shall have received its due, it must no longer
seek to lay its hand on literature, art, higher

education, pure science, philosophy, manners. And then, — when the mass of men are politically and economically free, — we must preserve the sacred fire of intellectual light by setting apart a priesthood, a body of intellectual men who shall worship the God of truth and him alone. Our professors at Harvard, Yale, and elsewhere, for instance, constitute, or should constitute, such a priesthood; but the public is not satisfied to have them serve the sacred flame: the public wishes them to apply that sacred flame to furnaces and dynamos. We do need, as Mr. Dickinson implies, intellectual traditions of generations of educated men; those traditions should be taught as a sacred cult; and their priests should be held in special reverence. Those priests should be most honored when they serve intellectual concerns in which the public sees no profit, such as philosophy and the classics. We do need, as a quickening fountain, in the midst of us, a spirit of reverence for intellectual beauty. Had such a spirit of reverence existed among us, should we have been so exposed to Mr. Lowes Dickinson's criticisms, and should we now be almost as remote from Goethe as from Dante or Plato?

THE CLASSICS AGAIN

A Dialogue Concerning the Loeb Classical Library [1]

BROWN, *a historian.*   JONES, *a clergyman.*
ROBINSON, *a dilettante*

Scene, Brown's apartment

BROWN; *enter* JONES

BROWN. — How d' do, Jones, delighted to see
you. I hope that you are very well.

JONES. — Very well, my dear boy, and you?
How are you getting on with your work? Have
you the German microscope under your eye? Are
you putting the atomic theory to use in history?

[*Enter* ROBINSON]

ROBINSON. — How d' do, how d' do? How
are you, parson? And how are you, Mommsen
Gregorovius Macaulay?

BROWN. — I have been loafing lately. I felt
the need of contrast, of looking about me a little

[1] The Loeb Classical Library. Edited by T. F. PAGE and
W. H. D. ROUSE.

164

at the actual world.   If one does not turn away from dead records occasionally, one is in danger of forgetting that history professes to be a record of life.

JONES. — Does it ?   If the histories that I see record life, the world has been horribly dull. All past generations of Germans must have been delighted to die.   I dare say that history should be a record of life; it certainly should record enough of human experience to teach us, the living, what to do and what to let alone.   History ought to be of service; that is its justification.

ROBINSON. — Yes, service in a broad sense, that whatever adds an interest to life is serviceable. I don't mean to correct you, *mon vieux*, but I am afraid you are tarred with the notion of a moral interpretation of history.

JONES. — You can't avoid the moral interpretation of history, *mon cher*, unless you are willing to eliminate from our lives metaphysics, ethics, relig—

ROBINSON. — Gladly, gladly !

BROWN. — Have a cigar ?

[They take cigars and light them]

JONES *[picking up a book]*. — Hullo !   You, too, have got the Loeb Classical Library.   Have you looked at it ?

BROWN. — Yes, a little, at the first volumes that have come out.

ROBINSON. — I subscribed the other day. I have an empty shelf at the top of my bookcase that needs to be filled up. I call it my *Via Appia,* because I bury the classics there.

JONES. — Do you frequent it ?

ROBINSON. — I read them on Sunday mornings as an excuse for not attending your church.

JONES. — I'm more than glad to have you listen to louder preachers of piety than I am.

BROWN. — Seriously, how do you like them ? I mean do you think it worth while to republish the classics ?   This publication sounds like a challenge.

ROBINSON. — It is a challenge, a serious challenge. It raises the question of the worth of the classics in its broadest form.

JONES. — You mean the value of the classics in education as opposed to the value of science ?

ROBINSON. — No, although that question is included. This is a challenge, not from a man of science, but from a man who is interested in literature and professes a belief in the classics, demanding to know what we honestly, not professionally, not conventionally, but what, honor-bright, we think of the classics.   The Loeb Classical Library says as distinctly as a dozen or twenty published

volumes, with ten-score-odd to follow, can say:
"Come, you are no longer able to take refuge in
the inadequacy of your school and college; you
can no longer say that if you had but the necessary
time to polish up your Greek, to practise your
Latin, you would have Euripides in one pocket
and Lucretius in the other, and in odd moments
be gratifying your natural appetite for the classics.
You have no further excuses. Do you or do you
not care a rap about us?" Here is, indeed, an
embarrassing question for us who have always
upheld the classics with our lips, for it does not
come from the camp of the men of science, but
from our own friends. So long as the classics
were safely locked up in their Greek and Latin
cupboards, we were always able to defend ourselves with an "if." This hypothetical, and, it
is to be feared, sometimes hypocritical, defence,
is no longer open to us, now that the cupboards are
unlocked; we have but to turn the handle and we
shall be able to satisfy our hunger. Mr. Loeb has
done the cause of honesty a good turn. We can
no longer shuffle and evade, we must confront the
question, What do the classics mean to us?

BROWN. — Well, if this is a challenge, it is a
fair challenge. Mr. Loeb has taken a generous
view of the classics. His library, according to the

announcement, will contain not merely the literatures of ancient Greece and ancient Rome, but
also the literature of early Christianity, as well as
whatever there is of value and interest in later
Greek and Latin literature until the fall of Con-
stantinople.   So wide a range, shelf upon shelf,
eliminates whatever objections individual taste
might have raised to a narrower selection.

JONES. — Suppose that we were to take up the
challenge and endeavor to frame an answer to this
question.   Should we not first have to face the
preliminary question, what does literature in
general do for us?   Must not that question be
answered before we say just what the classical
literatures mean to us?

BROWN. — Well, let's see if we do not agree
on the value of literature in general.   In the first
place we all agree that life is a marvellous happen-
ing.   We find ourselves here in the midst of a vast
flux of forces.   Men of science bid us fit ourselves
for this wonderful experience by studying matter
and energy, the earth and its materials, the air,
gases, electricity, chemical activities, germs, all
the phenomena that touch our senses.   This is
sound advice; we human beings are frail creatures,
sensitive to the play of this infinite variety of
forces.   We feel, we suffer, we enjoy.   In fact our

intelligence is a contrivance of nature to protect
and guard our sensitiveness. Yet these forces
of nature, these mysterious gods, so potent in sky,
air, and earth, noble and terrible in lightning
and tempest, in comet and earthquake, in the very
great and the very little, manifest themselves still
more terribly and still more nobly in human form.
Our fellow men are the forces that make our life
a pleasure or a pain, a happiness or a vain thing.
From them come love, affection, sympathy, approbation, distrust, disapproval, hate. They are the
forms of energy that we need chiefly to study,
and as it is difficult to learn lessons from actual
life, it is important to study these human
energies in the past, where at our leisure we
can go over and over the record; there the results of causes are chronicled as well as the
causes themselves.

ROBINSON. — But you are talking of history,
not literature.

BROWN. — Literature is the only real history.
The main records of the past are not contained in
Gibbon, in Guizot, in Egyptian tombs, or in the
fossils of the Wind River beds, but in the books
of men who have recounted their experience of
life. From their experience we learn how best
to fulfil the duty of self-preservation.

ROBINSON. — You give literature a terribly utilitarian twist. You present the obverse of the Delphic motto, *Know Thyself;* you say, *Know Other Men.*

JONES. — Brown is right so far as he goes; but he stops short. Brown is too eager to meet the men of science on their own ground; he forgets what we of the cloth regard as more important than the body. The primary function of literature is to feed the soul.

ROBINSON. — The soul is a matter of metaphysics; but literature is a part of our earth, it grows in the ground like an oak. Define what you mean.

JONES. — I can't; the soul won't submit to definition. It is illimitable. It is as much a yearning as anything else. On the one hand it comes into relation with God, on the other to matter. It's relation to material things is to take what they have to give, to nourish itself by that taking, to feed on love, on self-purification, to grow strong by detaching itself from hate, from vulgarity, from grossness. The preservation of the soul is quite as important as the preservation of the body, and it needs not only the robust food offered by daily life, but the daintier food, often more nourishing, more invigorating, of literature.

For in literature the souls of men express themselves with more freedom and greater clearness
than they do in actual life.   It is hard to express
the soul in deeds; for life offers many hinderances,
and the deeds of the soul are often blurred by the
trivial or gross happenings of life, so that they no
longer exhibit the qualities of the soul, whereas
in literature the soul has been able to reveal itself
most completely.   So I value literature chiefly
as the record of human souls.   A knowledge of
spiritual life in others helps my own spiritual life.

ROBINSON. — That may apply to Thomas-à-
Kempis or the *Vita Nuova*, but how about *Madame
Bovary*, or *Il Fuoco*?

JONES. — The records of a sick soul, of a dying
soul, teach lessons as well as the records of a
healthy soul.   The pathology of the soul is a
necessary part of spiritual knowledge.

ROBINSON. — You fellows take professional
views.   Your wits have been subdued to your
callings.   Life is not an endeavor to attain or to
ward off, it is a matter of entertainment; it is
neither a school nor a chapel, it is a theatre.
Melancholy Jaques said the last word on that
subject.   Men and women are players, endlessly
playing tragedy, comedy, farce, or more commonly
a piece composed of all three.   We must look at

life objectively. The spectator's business is to interest himself in the plot, to welcome the thrill of tragedy, to smile at the comic, to laugh at the farcical, and all the time to take his presence at the play as a privilege, to value the lighted theatre far higher than the unknown without, where there is neither light nor sound. Literature is the record of past life. It is a play within the play and to be taken at the same estimate as life, as an opportunity for a most varied entertainment.

BROWN. — If our views are professional, your view is the most professional of all. This universe as we see it, the result of toil, patience, energy, beyond the reach of man's imagination —

ROBINSON. — Exists for the sake of the dilettante. Precisely; there is no other possible hypothesis.

JONES. — Well, let us not wander too far from the subject. How does all this apply to the three literatures that Mr. Loeb has gathered together for the sake of challenging us?

II

BROWN. — Our opinions of literature are, as I understand them, of this general purport. Literature, according to me, shows us the nature of our fellow men; that is, it portrays those manifestations of force which most affect us during our pilgrimage through life, and therefore enables us to use those forces to our advantage or to prevent them from doing us hurt. According to Jones, literature, being in its deepest sense the tale of the spiritual experiences of men, of the success or failure of the human soul, teaches us how to educate our own souls. Or, if we follow Robinson, and regard life primarily as a spectacle, then literature adds immensely to the richness of the show by supplementing the incompleteness of the present with the greater completeness of the past, and so adds to the value of life.

If we commit ourselves to these principles, how do we apply them to the three literatures which the first volumes of the Loeb Classical Library present to our attention; how, to begin with, to the literature of early Christianity? That seems to fall rather more in your province, Jones, than in ours. What do you think of the volumes of the Apostolic Fathers and of St. Augustine?

JONES. — I fear I shall have to begin, as I used to begin my lectures at the theological school, with some general statements. Will you please bear with me, Robinson?

ROBINSON. — Reverie, if not sleep, is always open to me.

JONES. — Christianity is the fruit of the maternal tenderness in humanity; it was born of the great throbs of compassion for mortal sorrows, and at birth dedicated itself to the ennoblement of mankind, for in ennoblement, as it believed, lies our only hope of happiness. The first disciples were sensitive men, ignorant of, or indifferent to, the pleasures of the world, who rejoiced in the belief that self-sacrifice for an ideal is the solution of life's enigma. The history of the beginning of Christianity is the most famous literature in our western world, and, I suppose, fulfils Robinson's requirements as well as Brown's and mine.

In that first period of Christian history the sacred fire was lighted. In the second period the task was of a different order; that second task was to keep the sacred fire alive, and so, in order to protect it from the winds and rain, the disciples of the first disciples built about it the great edifice of the Church. In the book of the Apostolic Fathers, which contains the Epistles of Clement, of Ignatius, and of Polycarp, this devout process is plainly at work. [*Jones goes to the table and picks up* "The Apostolic Fathers."] The scene is in the Roman Empire, the time is at the end of the first and the beginning of the second century, and

yet we are at once aware that we have left the
precincts of the ancient world and have entered
the purlieus of the Middle Ages. There, before
us, crowned with light or darkness, as you may
please to think, rises the mighty fabric of the
Holy Roman Church. Certainly, my dear Robinson, by this event the theatre of history was greatly
enriched.

ROBINSON. — The early Christians make a most
interesting episode. But you must not exaggerate their piety. The Emperor Hadrian, who was
inclined, like me, to look upon life as a theatre,
wrote to his friend Servianus a few words about
the Christians in Egypt. "Egypt, which you
praised to me so warmly, my dear Servianus, I
found altogether frivolous, unstable, and shifting
with every breath of rumor. Their one god is
money; him, Christians, Jews, and Gentiles alike
adore."

JONES. — The emperor was looking for diversion
and failed to get anything more than diversion;
and so when he wished to satisfy his longing for
beauty, for an element of poetry in life, he could
rise no higher than to gaze at Antinous. The
Christians of Egypt may have adored Mammon,
but there were Christians in Syria and Asia
Minor who did not. Here in this book is proof.

It contains poetry, exquisite poetry ; it asserts that
poetry is the order of the universe, that poetry
is truth.   It is worth while, in our search after
nourishment for the soul, to come upon men who
believe this.   In actual life there may be many
such people, but they are hard to find; those
who live poetry are, in my experience, very
shamefaced about it.   Let me read you this.
[*Reads from Clement.*]   "The heavens moving
at his appointment are subject to Him in
peace ; " — but no, that is too long, I will merely
read you his prayer.

"Grant us to hope on thy name, the source of all
creation, open the eyes of our heart to know thee,
that thou alone art the highest in the highest, and
remainest holy among the holy.   Thou dost
humble the pride of the haughty, thou dost
destroy the imaginings of nations, thou dost raise
up the humble and abase the lofty, thou makest
rich and makest poor, thou dost slay and make
alive, thou alone art the finder of spirits and art
God of all flesh, thou dost look on the abysses,
thou seest into the works of man, thou art the
helper of those in danger, the saviour of those in des-
pair, the creator and watcher over every spirit. . . .
Save those of us who are in affliction, have mercy
on the lowly, raise the fallen, show thyself to those

in need, heal the sick, turn again the wanderers
of thy people, feed the hungry, ransom our pris-
oners, raise up the weak, comfort the faint-hearted;
let all 'nations know thee, that thou art God
alone,' and that Jesus Christ is thy child, and that
we are thy people, and the sheep of thy pasture."

Is there not something to be learned from people
whose life is centred in poetry? Does not their
idea of what is worth while teach us something,
which we, looking about us, would not be able
to find for ourselves? Do we not need, in a world
preoccupied with chemistry, physics, biology, to
remember that many men have found extraordinary help in prayer? Listen to this: "Love
of joy and of gladness," says the epistle of Barnabas, "is the testimony of the works of righteous-
ness." "None of these things [sundry duties to
be done] are unknown to you if you possess perfect
faith towards Jesus Christ, and love, which are the
beginning and end of life; for the beginning is
faith and the end is love, and when the two are
joined together in unity, it is God, and all other
noble things follow after them. No man who
professes faith sins, nor does he hate who has
obtained love." On these wings the early Christians flew high above poverty, sickness, oppression, envy, and meanness; they found the key

N

that unlocked for them the riches of life; they
discovered what we are all seeking; they became,
as Barnabas says, τέκνα εὐφροσύνης, Children of
Mirth. If a knowledge of early Christian literature will help us to learn from them, there is
something to be said for it.

ROBINSON. — I agree that the picture of these
men dragging their chains from Antioch to Rome,
merely fearful lest some untoward chance should
deprive them of the joy of being devoured by
wild beasts, is highly melodramatic. The Roman
amphitheatre has claims on the gratitude of
posterity.

BROWN. — The interest really lies in the singular power that these men displayed. Here is a
belief-engendered energy that shames the dynamo.
Polycarp had a countless line of ancestors, stretching immeasurably back to the beginnings of
organic life on this globe, and each parent in that
countless line transmitted to his child one great
duty, to shun death; and for unnumbered generations every child obeyed, until there in Antioch,
Polycarp, under the influence of a fantastic belief,
broke that primal law as if it had been a dry twig.
In fact, these Christians claimed to control a very
potent form of energy, and their method of
exercising that control was by prayer. This is a

matter of psychological interest; we cannot study this power too closely, nor can we make too many experiments in the hope of becoming able to draw upon it at will.   I think that Jones is making out a good case for his view of the value of literature.

JONES. — As I seem to have the floor, I will go ahead with this other book, these two red volumes, *The Confessions of St. Augustine*, which in point of history constitutes another stage in the development of Christianity. The pages, it is true, contain a great mist of rhetorical piety (if that phrase is not too unsympathetic); but out of this mist every now and again emerge some human details, with the peculiar charm that bits of landscape have when a fog lifts and the greens of field and wood shine in summer sunlight. St. Augustine certainly has not neglected to gratify Robinson's taste for the theatre. But the real significance of the *Confessions* lies in its contribution to our understanding of the soul. Will you bear with me while I read a little more?

BROWN. — Fire away.

JONES. — The twelfth chapter of the eighth book recounts Augustine's retreat to a garden after a struggle between the Spirit and the Flesh. It tells how a rush of emotion overcame him, how he flung himself down under a fig tree and

cried out between his sobs : [*reads*] "And then, O
Lord, how long, how long, Lord, wilt thou be
angry? for ever? Remember not our former
iniquities (for I found myself to be still enthralled
by them). Yea, I sent up these miserable excla-
mations, How long? how long still, 'to-morrow
and to-morrow'? Why not now? Wherefore
even this very hour is there not an end put to my
uncleanness?" Then he heard a young voice,
like a boy's or girl's, say in a sort of chant, "Tolle,
lege, — Take up, and read," So he went back
to the apostle's book and read, "Put ye on the
Lord Jesus Christ, and make not provision for the
flesh, to fulfil the lusts thereof." He needed to
read no further, "for instantly . . . all the darkness
of doubting vanished away." His friend, Alypius,
hearing of Augustine's experience, shares in its
effect. They go to Monica, — *Inde ad matrem
ingredimur, indicamus: gaudet.* There is a simplicity and directness in the Latin that is ill-
rendered by "From that place we went to my
mother and told her. She was overjoyed."

And if any one is impatient to learn, in the space
of a single page, the cause of the triumph of
Christianity, let him turn to the tenth chapter of
the ninth book, where Augustine and Monica,
while they wait at Ostia for a ship to carry them

home to Carthage, commune with one another on their religion, leaning out of the window that looked into the garden. They are considering what the Gospel means by the words, "Enter thou into the joy of thy Lord." I use my own translation in part. Saint Augustine says: [*reads*]

"Suppose that the tumult of the flesh be still, that the phantasm of the earth, the waters, the air, and the heavens be silent, that the soul itself be silent, and by not thinking of itself transcend itself, that dreams be silent and all the revelations of the imagination, and every tongue and every sign; suppose that every moving thing be silent altogether (for, if any one listen, all things say, we have not made ourselves, but He that is everlasting made us). Suppose, after they have said this, that they keep silent, since they have lifted up our ears to Him that made them, and that He speak alone, not by them but of Himself, so that we hear his voice, not by tongue of flesh, neither by voice of angel, nor by sound of thunder, nor by the riddle of allegory, but that we hear Him, whom in his creatures we love, that we hear Him without them — just as we now reach out and by swift thought touch the eternal wisdom that overspreads all things. Suppose that this exaltation of soul continue, and that all visions that are not in keeping be taken away, but this vision ravish the seer, swallow him up, and immerse him in inward joy, so that his life forever shall be such as was his moment of understanding, for which we have yearned. Is not this: Enter thou into the joy of thy Lord?"

BROWN. — You are right. Such lives are lessons in the largest sense. What you have read is not merely the meditation of a philosopher, pondering over an hypothesis that the mind might entertain, but a vital, creative energy sprung from a particular, definite belief. Such a life as his gives significance to metaphysics. Here is a force as little understood as radium or the magnetic pole, and it seems to have a greater power than they; Augustine's belief dominated his life, and through him dominated a world, bringing nobleness and joy. I quite agree with you, Jones.

ROBINSON. — As a spectator, I applaud. Had Augustine not lived, my seat in this singular playhouse would have been of less value.

III

BROWN. — After all, the pagan classics of Rome and Greece constitute the bulk of the Loeb Library. It is they that ask, "What do we mean to you?"

JONES. — I suppose that you have in mind their direct influence upon us; for indirectly, we all admit, they have affected us enormously.

BROWN. — Yes, their direct effect upon us.

ROBINSON. — Unfortunately, they have no *direct* effect upon us.

JONES. — Because we neglect them?

ROBINSON. — No; but because with our inheritance, we cannot, or at least do not, look upon the classics with our own eyes.

BROWN. — Explain yourself.

ROBINSON. — We are children of the Italian Renaissance. That movement, so far as it concerns the classical world, was an interpretation; and the interpretation that the Renaissance adopted has been handed down to us. This tradition has determined how we shall look, how we shall see, what, in short, our conception of the Greek and Latin classics shall be.

JONES. — You are not speaking of scholars, are you?

ROBINSON. — No; I speak of the conventional conception of the classics entertained by persons who are not scholars. Scholars have their own academic conventions concerning the classics, contrived by Selden, Porson, Jebb, and their coadjutors of Paris, Leipsic, and Berlin; with that I have nothing to do. I refer to the definite, conventional conception of the classics that has become a part of our western culture. This conception was shaped for us by the Italians of the Renaissance. To them the great world of Rome, of law, of culture, of civilization, that lifted its distant head above the coarse, inane happenings of the Middle Ages, was a golden time — *Saturnia regna;* it appeared to them as the Alps first appeared to young Ruskin, rising in snow-capp'd, inaccessible glory. In this matter, we are disciples of the Renaissance. We dress our minds in clothes of its fashioning. Dante's invocation to Virgil, in the wild wood in which he had lost his way,

Or se' tu quel Virgilio?

is, as it were, the first modern cry of greeting to the great figures of the ancient world. Then follows Petrarch's adoration of Cicero, and Boccaccio's eulogy of Rome. All the stirrings of the Italian mind turned toward the mighty past of Rome. From Italy this Italian conception of the classics spread to the north. France took fire. On and on the admiration of the achievements of antiquity proceeded, invading England and Germany; and finally in the eighteenth century it burst out again with renewed power.

But, as you know, Brown, far better than I, of all this multitude of admirers, imitators, and eulogists of the classical world, those who have had most effect in fashioning our popular idea of what that world means, are the great Germans, Winckelmann, Lessing, and Goethe. They, more than the others, justified the tradition and imposed upon us the conception that the antique world was compact of sobriety, poise, measure, and proportion, qualities that we find crammed into our word "classical." Lessing says, somewhere, "It was the happy privilege of the ancients never to pass beyond or stop short of the proper limit." Winckelmann expressed the same idea, and Goethe spent a lifetime seeking to impress this same conception upon conduct. "A man," he says, "may accomplish much through directing individual abilities to one goal; he may accomplish the unusual through the union of several capacities; but the wholly unpredictable, the *Unique*, he achieves only if all his powers unite together in even measure. The last was the happy lot of the Ancients, especially the Greeks of the best time."

BROWN. — Nevertheless, in spite of Goethe's reference to the Greeks, in spite of Winckelmann's and Lessing's belief that they were holding up

Greek models to the world, in spite of the French classical tragedy, or the universal admiration of Homer, the meaning of the word "classical" for them was Latin, not Greek.

JONES. — That is true, of course.

BROWN. — Therefore, although sobriety, measure, repose, are contained in our word classical, there is a definiteness, a circumscription, a conventionality, a practicality, in the phrase, that could only have come from Latin influence. Our conception of the classics is Latin or at best Græco-Latin. If the shapers of the classical tradition had been bred upon Greece instead of upon Rome, they never would have attempted to cram the meaning of ancient Greece into a conception which could be represented by a single phrase, even when that phrase — sobriety, measure, repose — has so much convenience to recommend it. You agree to this, Robinson, don't you?

ROBINSON. — Oh, yes; you are perfectly right. My point was that we accept the classics upon a wholly traditional valuation; and I was going to add that one of the great services which Mr. Loeb's classical library renders is that we are morally obliged to look at the classics, so far as it is possible, with our own eyes and make up our own minds about them. We must take the word classical down from its pedestal and see what it really means.

JONES. — You were quite right, Robinson, to call our attention to this tradition, but you have digressed from the point. Let us get back to the subject we started with : What do these Greek and Latin classics mean to us ?

ROBINSON. — Excuse me, parson, but I meant to remove an obstacle from our path.

JONES. — It is for me, sir, to apologize; you were wholly right. Unluckily the clock warns me that we have gone past half our time.

IV

BROWN. — We all agree, I suppose, that the study of poise, measure, sobriety, self-control, would be of great advantage to us. And if tradition, no matter how it originated, ascribes to the literature of Greece and Rome those qualities, it is worth while to consider the matter and find out if there be any truth in that tradition.

I think that a hasty glance at Greek literature will contradict tradition very flatly, and show that these traits were no more characteristic of the Greeks as human beings, than of ourselves. [*Goes to bookcase and takes down one or two books.*] Take Homer, and you see that the Greeks acted under the push of passion with the energy of their southern temperament. When Achilles is angry with Agamemnon he says: "Thou heavy with wine, thou with face of dog and heart of deer." And when he has struck down Hector of the glancing plume, he spurns his entreaties: "Entreat me not, dog, by knees or parents. Would that my heart's desire could so bid me myself to carve and eat raw thy flesh, for the evil thou hast wrought me, as surely there is none that shall keep the dogs from thee, not even should they bring ten or twentyfold ransom and here weigh it out, and promise even more; not even were Priam, Dardano's son, to bid pay thy weight in gold, not even so shall thy lady mother lay thee on a bed to mourn her son, but dogs and birds shall devour thee utterly." And after Hector is dead, "Other sons of the Achaians ran up around, who gazed upon the stature and marvelous goodliness of Hector. Nor did any stand by but wounded him, and thus would many a man say looking toward his neighbor: 'Go to, of a truth far easier to handle is Hector now than when he burnt the ships with blazing fire.' Thus would many a man say, and wound him as he stood hard by."

Achilles is a passionate child, and the Homeric Greeks an emotional, excitable people. In Soph-

ocles, you remember how the mad Ajax is described as mistaking sheep for his enemies. "Of
part, he cut the throats on the floor within;
some, hewing their sides, he rent asunder. Then
he caught up two white-footed rams; he sheared
off the head of one, and the tongue-tip, and flung
them away; the other he bound upright to a pillar,
and seized a heavy thong of horse-gear, and flogged
with shrill, double lash, while he uttered revilings
which a god, and no mortal, had taught."

The *Trojan Women* is one long wail, and *Phil-
octetes* is almost as full of self-pity as *Obermann*.
Even the aphorisms of Sophocles are often as
intemperate as the utterances of the Hebrew
prophets:

"Searching out all things, thou in most men's
acts wilt find but baseness."

"A woman's oaths I write upon the waves."

"Man is but breath and shadow, nothing more."

JONES. — How about the lyric poets?

BROWN. — From Archilochus to Bion there is
passionate intensity. Passion can never be temperate, it forgets all else and concentrates itself
on its own piercing sensation; that was true of the
Greeks as of all hot-blooded human beings —

ROBINSON. — I suppose that those early Italians really based their classical formula on archi-

tecture, on the Greek temple and the Roman arch, and on sculpture, much more than on literature.

JONES. — Critics have always confounded the arts; they apply terms of painting to music, of music to architecture, of architecture to literature, and call their confusion criticism.

BROWN. — Poor fellows! Perhaps you need not put them all into one category. But Robinson is right, I think, in assuming that the traditional idea of Greek literature has been taken from Greek sculpture and architecture. The makers of the tradition did not know Greek literature. You cannot compress the Greeks' expression of their experience of life into a single formula. Professor Wheeler says that Æschylus is "mystic and transcendental"; Professor Shorey that "the antithesis of classical and realistic is as false as the opposition of classic and romantic." Mr. Gilbert Murray speaks of the "terrible emotional" power possessed by Thucydides; and in another passage he warns us of the danger of serious misapprehension that lies in inferences based upon the judgment of the scribes who selected but a small portion of the great mass of Greek literature for preservation. [*Takes up magazine and reads*]: "When one reads accounts in textbooks of the characteristics of the Greek mind: its statuesque quality, its love of proportion and order and common sense, its correct rhetoric and correct taste, its anthropomorphism and care for form, and all those other virtues which sometimes seem, when added together, to approach so dangerously near the total of dull correctness and spiritual vacuity, it is well to remember that the description applies not to what the ancient Greeks wrote, but to what the late Roman and Byzantine scholars preserved."

ROBINSON. — How about Latin literature? You stated that the tradition of classical sobriety, so far as it is based on literature at all, is based much more on the Latin classics than on the Greek? Perhaps Latin will justify, at least to some extent, the traditional view.

BROWN. — I can see no better ground for the tradition with regard to Latin than to Greek. Italian tradition having assumed that the ancient Roman character was like the masonry of the Colosseum, went further and assumed that Latin literature must have depicted it as such. But if we go behind the tradition and look directly at the Latin literature which depicts Roman character, we find that the ancient Romans were very much like ourselves, with no more poise, measure, sobriety, or repose than we Americans of to-day possess, if indeed as much. They were men like ourselves. Terence's famous line,

Homo sum: humani nil a me alienum puto,

sums up, as well as is possible in a single line, our two modern characteristics, human curiosity and human sympathy. Terence's *dramatis personæ* have no suggestion of brick, travertine, or mortar. Take the familiar lines of Catullus,

Vivamus, mea Lesbia, atque amemus,
Rumoresque senum severiorum
Omnes unius æstimemus assis.

Let us live, my Lesbia, and love,
And all the carping of stern old men
Let us rate at a penny's worth.

Read the verses in which Propertius bids his fellow-poet Gallus beware of falling in love with Cynthia,

Non ego tum potero solacia ferre roganti,

Were you then to come in supplication, I could not console you.

And again, take his complaint,

Me mediæ noctes, me sidera prona jacentem,
Frigidaque Eoo me dolet aura gelu.

I lie prostrate, pitied by midnight, by the setting stars
And the air cold with the frost of morning.

Or, since Propertius fills one of the first volumes in the Loeb Classical Library, read the beautiful

last farewell of Cornelia, daughter of Cornelius
Scipio, to her husband Paullus,

> Fungere maternis vicibus, pater.
> You, Father, must fill a mother's place.

Evidently the Romans had the same affections
and passions as we moderns. The verses of
Tibullus to Delia tell the same tale:

> Te videam suprema mihi cum venerit hora:
> Te teneam moriens deficiente manu!
> Thee shall I look at when my last hour comes;
> Thee, as I die, my failing hand shall hold.

ROBINSON. — But, if you disregard the meaning
and listen only to the words, you find a dignity, a
massiveness, in the Latin syllables that modern
literature seldom or never has.

BROWN. — There you come close to the cause
of the tradition. Compare Italian with Latin
and you perceive why the humanists of the
Renaissance found poise, measure, sobriety, and
repose in classical literature.

JONES. — I am a little confused. Am I to
understand that you wholly reject the tradition of
poise, measure, sobriety and self-control, as having
no affinity with classical literature?

BROWN. — Not at all. The tradition, begun
by the Italians of the Renaissance, is based on a
false analogy to sculpture and architecture, and

o

on the contrast between our modern Romance
languages and Latin; but I believe that those
qualities, though they do not lie in the character
or disposition of the ancients, are qualities of
their method of expression.

V

ROBINSON. — Translation is the work of a
hod-carrier. It carries from one language to
another only the grosser parts that can be loaded
and ferried across; it leaves behind both form and
color. Mathematics are the same in German,
Italian, and English; but the simplest word has
an individuality as marked as that of a human
child. To the ears of familiarity and affection
no other sequence of syllables can reproduce the
tenderness of the mother tongue. By means of
the Loeb Classical Library the reader of little
Latin and less Greek has an opportunity to turn
from the English and pick up a phrase or two, a
word, perhaps, here and there; merely to do so
puts him in the spiritual presence of the original.
He is then, as it were, reading about a person's
experiences, with the privilege at any moment
of looking up to see that person's face.

JONES. — That is true; but our question is,
how do the classics themselves help us?

ROBINSON. — The answer lies in one little word, *art*. The classics, more than any modern literature, teach us art, and art is the conscious purpose of man to make this world more beautiful. Philip Sidney says that the object of poetry is to make this too-much-loved world more lovely; I should extend his definition a little further and say that the object of art is to make this world more lovely, more lovable, and more loved.

Modern literature, compared with ancient literature, is careless, slipshod, not wholly grown-up; it has little sense of responsibility. The chief duty it sets before itself is to hold the mirror up to nature and reflect the unintelligible happenings of life, in all their confusion, their inconsistency, their inanity. Ancient literature was dominated by a very different purpose, it had a profound sentiment of high duty. The creation, so it seemed to the ancients, had been left incomplete, and man, as the creature most divine, was charged with the labor of carrying on the uncompleted task. With bold hearts the Greeks set to work to piece out the incompleteness with literature, especially with poetry, to make up for the neglect of the gods by human achievement. I look on those ancient Greeks and Romans as I do on workmen who fill in the marshy shallows of our river fronts, put earth upon the spongy ooze, sow grass, set out trees, plant flowers, and create a garden where before was merely mud and slime.

BROWN. — Life, as Wordsworth said, and I am glad to see that Robinson supports him, requires an art, and of all the arts the art of living is the most useful, the most admirable. All conscious art is an attempt to transfer emotion or thought from him who feels or thinks it to other human beings. Art is the necessary consequence of human sympathy. Men are not happy in isolation; they undergo the experience of emotion, of thought, and they are impelled to impart this wonderful experience to others. Some men make use of marble or bronze, some of pencil and paint, some of written signs. But more primitive, more fundamental, incomparably more wide reaching, as means to impart emotion and thought, are manners and speech. I hardly know which of the two is more important. By manners I mean the bearing of the body, in every part, from head to foot, the whole outward man. Our human instinct, the inner impulse, the will to live, insists, for one purpose or another, upon our imparting emotion and thought; to do so well requires art, to do so excellently is a fine art. To pass on emotion and thought unimpaired in their first

vigor, in their first freshness, adds the life of each
to the lives of all; it increases, intensifies, and
expands all life. Feelings, thoughts, are seeds,
shaken from the parent stalk, that lodge and fruc-
tify in new soil. Each feeling, each thought,
should pass on as free as light from mind to mind.
This art — the human art I may call it — lies in
the choice of words, in putting them in sequence,
in laying stress, in what Petrarch calls *il bel tacere*,
the art of silence, and in holding and moving
the body, — eyes, lips, arms, hands — so that
mind shall communicate with mind, free from
obscurity or blur, as through an open window.

Art is all one. We talk of the fine arts; but
that is an arbitrary distinction. Our abilities
and our time are limited, and naturally we give
ourselves up to that form of art which seems most
suited to our purposes; but one thing we are all
bound to do, and that is to remain stanchly
loyal to all art. The Greeks were the supreme
artists, and we must go to them as to the fountain :
head of the waters which alone can quench the
human thirst for human sympathy. They teach
us how best to live. By studying delicacy,
beauty, power, clarity, in their written speech,
we learn how much those qualities add to the
fulness of life, and we take away a humble desire

to do our best to render our own lives, and the lives of our friends, fuller, more complete, more in accord with the possibilities of life.

ROBINSON. — Yes. As Brown was saying, the special qualities, sobriety, self-control, repose, which tradition assigns to the classics, although not true of Greek or Latin feelings, are in great measure true of the form in which those feelings are expressed in Greek and Latin literature. Tradition is wrong to attribute those utterly non-southern qualities to living Greeks and Romans, but it is right to recognize that they are the chief qualities in classical form. Form is the legacy of antiquity to us. Life is movement, it does not concern itself with form. Life at its best, at its highest, is passion. Passion is the one sacred quality that exists, so far as man can see, in the universe. The chief duty of art is to per-petuate passion by putting it in such form that all who behold shall be quickened and take away more life and fuller. The ancients learned that the only way to represent passion is through re-straint; that sobriety and measure offer the least imperfect means to depict life in its intensity.

That is the lesson of art for the theatre, as Hamlet knew before me. That is the lesson that Brown clamors for, the lesson of conduct. To

learn it we must go to school to the classics. If
the Loeb Classical Library helps us to comprehend
the immense significance of restraint in the delineation of life, it has achieved a great thing.

JONES. — I have much in common with both
of you, but, probably because I am a clergyman,
my point of view is a little different. I advocate
the classics because they constitute a retreat, in
which the spirit may commune with the high
thoughts of the past. Modern literature is
modern; it concerns itself with actual life, with
our distractions, our trivialities, our romance,
our getting on in the world, with all our coarser
appetites; but in the remote classics, in that cool,
tranquil, distant world, we can surrender ourselves to contemplation, to meditation, to the high
influences that always stoop to the soul's call.

This remoteness of the classics affects me as my
remembrance of gracious figures in my childhood.
The people there seem to have a nobler aspect,
a more goodly presence, larger sympathies, a
wiser and a kinder attitude. We do not apply
the lessons we learned from them directly to life,
but we know that somehow the most valuable
lessons in our lives came from them; we cannot
say just what we learned, but we possess a memory
of quietness, of ripeness, of wisdom, of qualities

that lie near the centre of life, and we feel that to them is due whatever gain we have made in grace and moral stature. Greek literature has a like effect upon us.

We need, profoundly, times of seclusion, of withdrawal from the outer world, from the domination of the senses; we need to escape from the current notion that life lies in motion, in rush, in physical activity. We need a contradictory force, an opposing experience. We can no longer betake ourselves to a Carthusian monastery or a Benedictine abbey: the East is too strange, too little akin to us; but the classics of Greece and Rome offer us a retreat, a refuge for the tired spirit, a home for the unquiet mind. I, for one, long to put on from time to time cowl, cord, and sandals, and dwell in the sequestered and cloistered classics, far from the senseless noises of the world.

As to art, I agree that the classics teach it, that we need it, that self-expression is or should be an art; and for me the function of this art of self-expression is to reveal the more delicate, the more subtle, the more spiritual elements of the soul. Many people, I believe, possess fine qualities, but because of inability to master their medium of expression, whether act, word or silence, those qualities, as Shakspere says, "die to themselves." To preserve these tender blossoms of the soul, and to transmit their sweetness, is one of the problems of religion, a problem that needs the help of art. Without great art, conscious or unconscious, the self-revelation of all great spiritual souls would have been impossible. David, if the psalms are his, St. Augustine, Thomas à Kempis, John Bunyan, Jonathan Edwards, are great artists. More than all other people the Greeks possessed the art of portraying the finer qualities of the soul, as well as the "deep and dazzling darkness" that encompasses humanity.

ROBINSON. — The business of art — I merely add this in order to define my own position — is not merely to quicken all life, to heighten its pulse, by means of a fuller and freer intercommunication of thought and feeling. Art must always be up and at work, refashioning the things of the earth for the good of man. Architecture can make a city beautiful, sculpture and painting can add their loveliness; but those arts merely concern things material. Literature has a greater duty. Literature must take the stuff that human experience is made of, work upon it, and convert it into nobler, more beautiful, more stimulating shapes. Literature must tear away the curtain of familiarity that hides the beauty in common things. Or, as Parson Jones would put it, literature is the angel, the æon, the demiurge, that redeems this gross life and helps wipe out its shame. Would you rather see the England in which the men Shakspere, Chaucer, Wordsworth actually lived, or that England as they, as poets, have pictured it? Would you rather have lived in France under Louis Philippe, in Russia under Alexander II, or as Balzac and Tolstoï described the one and the other? I find all life chaotic until it has passed through the mind of an artist.

JONES. — Robinson grows lyrical. That means that it is very late, and time to go to bed. Good night, Brown.

ROBINSON. — Who cares for what the isles of Greece were to the common men who lived in them? But the realms of gold, which Æschylus, Sappho, Theocritus created, are still the home of beauty.

JONES. — Come on, Robinson. You are a literary Niobe, all words.

BROWN. — Good night. Come again.

ROBINSON. — Good night. My last word is Greece.

LITERATURE AND COSMOPOLITANISM

I

READERS of literature who entertain a fond belief that literature emancipates the human spirit, especially those who read European books in the belief that they are opening their souls as well as their minds, and that by training themselves upon things cosmopolitan they are shaking off the narrow bonds of national prejudice, have suffered a cruel shock. In this bloody upheaval of Europe, where all men are in dire need of temperance, serenity, and an emancipated spirit, the leaders of European literature are swept off their feet by the flood of national passion, just as madly as statesmen, news-vendors, fishmongers, merchants, and all who constitute the national mob. Is the "Republic of Letters" as much the home of fanaticism, of the negation of reason, of mad self-love, as a military barrack? Is there no medicine in literature to heal the mind sick with national egotism? Or are the present chiefs of European letters — Hauptmann, Maeterlinck, and the rest — not worthy of the respect in which the world has held them?

The "Republic of Letters" is an idea so covered with lichens of respectability that it has become an object of vague homage, and is commonly believed to possess wonder-working properties. To it has been assigned not merely the large and serene duty of instilling respect for letters in all those who waste their powers in getting and spending, but also that of spreading democracy, of substituting peace for war, of playing a part at least as great as that hoped for from Christianity. The "Republic of Letters" is to break down the barriers between nations, pull up ancient landmarks, and establish a human *patria*. Several considerations have aided this notion. In the Renaissance, at which school our modern world acquired the complexion of its thought, all that was then acknowledged as literature — the classics of Greece and Rome — was termed the humanities; and Terence's apothegm, *homo sum, humani nil a me alienum puto*, was weighted with new solidity. In this realm of the spirit every human being could find a home. The power of the humanities seemed herculean; as soon as the things of the mind were recognized to be the real things of life, political boundaries, national

jealousies, race-prejudices, would vanish of themselves, and the problem of inhumanity be solved.
This idea we have inherited.

Besides this, in the "Republic of Letters" a
succession of men have risen to the office of supreme authority, not by right of heredity, not as
representing God on earth, not at the will of
a Pretorian Guard or a military caste, but by
the universal suffrage of enfranchised minds in
all Europe. Plato, Cicero, Petrarch, Voltaire,
Goethe, are recognized as belonging to the
whole world; their great names knit up the
ravelled sleave of national divisions and bind all
peoples into one. Their influence spreads far
beyond the boundaries of their native states, and
unites men from east, west, north, and south, in
common discipleship.

Added to these grounds of hope that literature
would arouse in men a recognition of their common brotherhood, is the part played in the creation of literature by curiosity. At bottom natural
man is pure yokel, suspicious of men from another
village, afraid of travellers from afar; he builds a
wall to keep the alien world away. Nevertheless,
curiosity, the Ariel of the intellect, peers over the
wall into what tradition asserts is the Cimmerian
darkness beyond, and perceives something stirring.

After all, the people within the walls are not the only creatures that walk erect. Curiosity climbs over the wall and ventures to reconnoitre; it wanders on further and further, making discovery after discovery.

Literature is the noblest product of curiosity; we are curious to learn things outside ourselves. We wish to know the great deeds of our ancestors, how they fought the Trojans on the windy plains of Ilium; we wish to know about the covenant made by our fathers with their God, how they came out of the land of Egypt, and were led across the desert into the land of Canaan. We are eager to become acquainted with the ways and doings of our less immediate neighbors, — Becky Sharp, Père Goriot, Anna Karenina, Dorothea Casaubon, Hester Prynne.

This tendency to inquire concerning things beyond our village, beyond our province, operates also concerning things beyond our national boundaries. We are as inquisitive about life in London, Paris, or Rome, as about life in Boston or New York. We wish to learn foreign manners and customs, foreign ideas concerning all the multitudinous manifestations of life. We are as eager concerning things cosmopolitan as concerning things domestic, and we demand that literature shall tell us all about them. Curiosity in literature seems to take the direct road toward an international commonwealth.

Such facts as these have encouraged pacific men to a belief that literature might establish a cosmopolitanism which should make all men brothers, and do what Christianity and the Roman Catholic Church have failed to accomplish. And here and there, in rare instances, the idea of a world so concerned with matters of the mind that national discords fall like withered husks from the ripe fruit of the spirit, rises in majesty before some high and sensitive soul.

In the year 1870, by the eighth day of December, the Prussians had long been laying siege to the city of Paris. They had advanced from victory to victory: the Emperor of the French had surrendered at Sedan, Marshal Bazaine had surrendered at Metz. On that day, in the *Collège de France*, Gaston Paris, the famous teacher of mediæval literature, began his winter's course with a lecture on the *Chanson de Roland*.

He said, "I did not expect that I should reopen my course in the midst of this circle of steel that the German armies make round about us. Since I bade good-bye, in the month of June, to my kind audience, what strange things have happened!

Of those auditors who had already become for me
almost friends, very few doubtless are here again
to-day in this hall.   Some are taking part in the
defence of the city; others, unable to take a hand
therein, have gone to seek a little peace in foreign
lands; others, too, I cannot forget, are no doubt
in the very camp of the invaders."

Then he went on to say, —

"I do not think, in general, that patriotism has
anything to do with science.   The chairs of higher
learning are in no degree political platforms; they
are wrested from their true purpose if made to
serve, whether in defence or in attack, any end
whatever outside of their spiritual goal.

"I profess absolutely and without reserve this
doctrine, that learning has no other object than
truth, and truth for itself, without any heed of
consequences, good or bad, sorrowful or happy,
that truth may cause in practice.   He who from
any motive, patriotic, religious, or even ethical,
allows himself, in the facts which he studies or in
the conclusion which he draws, the smallest dis-
simulation, the very slightest alteration, is not
worthy to have his place in the great laboratory
where probity, as a title to admission, is more indis-
pensable than ability.

"So understood, studies in common, pursued

in the same spirit in all civilized countries, form above nationalities — which are limited, diverse, and too often enemies — a great *patrie* which no war soils, no conqueror menaces, and where souls find refuge and that union given them in ancient times by 'The City of God.'"

Nevertheless, this noble conception of a country beyond the greeds, the vulgar ambitions, the baser passions of man, does not point to a "Republic of Letters," but to a "Republic of Science." Science is the same for all men : the properties of numbers, the deductions of astronomers, the analyses of chemists remain the same whether the experiments are performed in Petrograd, Paris, or New York. Stars, rocks, radium, fossils, speak the same language to Swede and Spaniard, to Welshman and Serb. The sciences have one common mode of expression throughout the world; that mode is experiment. Sir Oliver Lodge, Ehrlich, Metchnikoff, Carrell, Flexner, Madame Curie, are all fellow laborers, — like so many carpenters, masons, and bricklayers, — busily at work upon the edifice of experimental truth. Their great tower ascends toward heaven ; and it will mount higher and higher, for no jealous god has cast upon the workmen the confusion of tongues.

P

Science has but one language, whereas thought which finds expression in literature is quite another matter. If literature embodied itself in some non-national medium, as numbers or musical notes, the whole weight of its influence would be in favor of brotherhood and unity. But, since the failure of Latin to maintain itself as a living language, literature has been dependent upon a medium which is the earliest and purest product of the national spirit, — language. Language is a steadfast assertion of national characteristics, national limitations, and national boundaries.

II

The spirit of literature finds its home in its native place. Literature must strike its roots into its native earth, and spread its branches to its native sunshine and its native breezes, or it will die. Literature is passionately patriotic; for it lives only in its native speech. Translate literature into another language, and instead of the living tree, its head lifted toward heaven, its branches spread wide over its native soil, you have cords of wood piled up in the market-place.

The great dictators of letters have dominated Europe through the power of national language, just as Cæsar spread his conquests by means of

Roman legions.   Plato is universal because in a
language unrivalled in its blending of intellectual
and sensuous qualities he embodied the Greek
spirit; in the English of Jowett he is something
quite other than himself.   Cicero, by a Roman
military splendor of rhetoric, by masterful control
of the stately phrases of Latin, filled the world
with his reputation.   Petrarch, indeed, succeeded
to the first place in European letters, because of
his lordship in every department of Latin literature, while Latin was still the universal language;
but within a hundred years, all those grounds for
his fame were forgotten, and he has since re-
mained enthroned because he is the greatest master of delicate expression in the Italian tongue.

Voltaire's renown throughout Europe was due
to his happy power of embodying the essence of
the Gallic genius in French prose.   Goethe, the
great apostle of cosmopolitanism, whose ideal was
to lift his head above the clouds and fog of
national discords, will surely, in the end, depend
for his glory upon his lyrical poems, for in them
he made exquisite use of what is best in the German heart and the German language.

The only name which absolutely transcends
national boundaries is that of Shakspere; but
who can say that even his delineation of the hu-

man soul in Hamlet, Othello, Lear, Cordelia,
Imogen, Shylock, could have won such world-
wide admiration, had it not been for his royal
power over Elizabethan English?

Read him at random:

There is a willow grows aslant a brook,
That shows his hoar leaves in the glassy stream;

.   .   .   .

There, on the pendent boughs her coronet weeds
Clambering to hang, an envious sliver broke;
When down her weedy trophies and herself
Fell in the weeping brook.

Is it not this Shaksperian English that constitutes
the wings of Shakspere's genius?

As all lovers of beauty were wont to make a
pilgrimage to Rheims because the cathedral there
was saturated with French genius; as we go to
Florence because the *Palazzo Vecchio*, Giotto's
campanile, and the pictured riches of the Uffizi,
are profoundly Italian; as we visit the yew-
shaded, tender-turfed, mellowed and memorial-
laden village churches of England, because they
breathe forth the very breath of England; so do
we betake ourselves to the great national classics
of literature.

The genius of a nation is the source of untold
riches; it has been bred by centuries, dandled by

favoring circumstances, nurtured and tutored by a thousand random influences; it has taken to itself a multitude of discordant elements, transformed them into a homogeneous whole, and stamped that whole with the national effigy and superscription.

Language is the most perfect expression of a nation's genius; it serves the nation's greatest needs; it has had the greatest labor bestowed upon it. Generation after generation has struggled to express in language its tenderest love, its profoundest passion, its bitterest grief, its most subtle thought. One man added a word here, another a phrase there; this man, as with a hammer, beat rough speech into smoothness and delicacy, a second rendered it pliable, a third fitted it for speculation. Mothers wrought it into a means of comforting their babies; lovers fashioned it into fantastic rhetoric of compliment; thinkers moulded it into a substance so light that it is hardly heavier than thought.

Finally, after a people has labored for centuries to create a national instrument, literature picks up that instrument and puts it to her uses. What literature shall do is determined by that instrument; she has no choice, she is the creature of her tool, she is the handiwork of language.

There was a time, hundreds of years ago, when cosmopolitanism dominated literature. The Latin language was but the spirit of the Roman Empire reincarnate in literature; the universal domination of one great people lived on in ghostly fashion. Even after national languages had long proved themselves amply sufficient for all the purposes of literature, brilliant spirits of the Renaissance — Ficino, Poliziano, Erasmus, — even Spinoza and Leibnitz, wrote in Latin; they wished to overstep national boundaries and write to all the world as fellow cosmopolites. And because they wrote in Latin, and not in their native languages, what they wrote belongs to the domain of thought, not to the domain of literature. Learning and the Church strove in vain to maintain Latin as a living language; it died just because it was cosmopolitan and in no wise national. Everywhere the power that carries literary fame throughout the world must be sought in some national trait.

We must not be disappointed to find that in this tumult of national passion these European men of letters became primitive, elemental, blinded by national egotism. Men of science, whose home is the laboratory, who talk in electrons and terms of energy; philosophers, who spend

their time in speculation concerning truth; statesmen, who know that under the promptings of greed
all nations behave like savages, — these have no
excuse for losing their moral equilibrium : physical
truth, philosophical truth, human nature, will not
be changed by the outcome of this war.   But it
may not be so with literature.   These men of
letters are instinctively right : literature, the
food of their souls, depends upon national spirit.
Literature would droop, decay, and become of no
more moral comfort to men than mathematics, if
it were to become cosmopolitan, or indifferent
to national existence.

III

Does literature then do nothing to soften men's
manners, to lift them to a large view of things, to
enable them to surmount the Chinese wall of
ignorance and prejudice which encircles every
nation, to crush in their hearts the brutal and
irrational war-spirit, to help bring about the long-
dreamed-of golden age of peace and good-will
among men ?   The answer is that, of course,
literature helps men in all these ways;   but not
by uprooting the instincts of patriotism.

Cicero's eulogy of the benefits conferred by
literature is as true to-day as on the day when he

defended Aulus Licinius Archias in the Roman forum. "*Haec studia adulescentiam alunt, senectutem oblectant, secundas res ornant, adversis perfugium ac solacium praebent, delectant domi, non impediunt foris, pernoctant nobiscum, peregrinantur, rusticantur.*" (These studies nourish youth, they delight old age, they add a grace to prosperity, they offer refuge and comfort in adversity, they are a pleasure at home, they are no trouble abroad, they will pass the night with us, accompany us on our travels, and stay with us in the country.)

All this is true. The benefits of literature can hardly be overestimated. Books enlarge a man's horizon. They raise a mirage of water-brooks and date-palms to travellers in a desert. They are "the sick man's health, the prisoner's release." Shut within a narrow routine of dull necessity, sad at heart in a world where wrong triumphs, where beauty has no assurance of respect, where humanity toils terribly merely for its daily bread or the satisfaction of trivial appetites, the earthly pilgrim need do no more than pick up a book, and lo! he steps forth into another world. Here he is free from sorrow and care, free from the burden of his body, from envy, jealousy, contempt, self-satisfaction, from vain regrets, from wishes that can never wear the livery of hope, from narrowness of soul and hardness of heart. He may mingle in the society of the good and great; he may listen to the wise man and the prophet; he may see all the conditions of human happiness and misery; he may watch the human spirit, in its strife with circumstance, nobly conquer or basely succumb; he may go down through the "gate of a hundred sorrows," or accompany Dante and Beatrice through the spheres of Paradise.

By means of literature we step from our narrow chamber into a brave world of unnumbered interests. After such experiences the reader acquires a larger view of life; in his heart he crushes the irrational and brutal war-spirit; he imagines for a season that men are brothers. And if this is true of readers who can leave their daily routine for the palace of literature but now and then, for an hour or two of an evening or on Sunday, it is far more true of the men who pass their lives in the palace and have contributed to its wonderful appurtenances.

The humanities do render men more humane; literature does fit them to be citizens of the world, without depriving them of their own homes. *Die versunkene Glocke, L'Oiseau bleu, Plays Pleasant and Unpleasant, Peter Pan, Jean Christophe,* all seem to be proofs of a broad and sensitive humanity.

But certainly Hauptmann, Maeterlinck, and their companions, swept away by national feeling, have given our world a shock. It is a natural disappointment; we had hoped that literature was an effective instrument of peace, and it comes with a sword. We are disappointed, not by what they have done, but by what they, or some among them, have left undone. Men whose country is threatened with destruction are right to cry out and fight for the preservation of their country, and men of letters more than others, for literature has rendered their own country still dearer to them than it is to other men. So far as their passion limits itself to the preservation of their own country, all the world will applaud them; if they overstep that limit and support, or justify, any attempt to destroy another nation, or if they remain silent during any such attempt, no matter who makes it, they are false to literature, as well as to civilization and to the nobler spirit of man. All these distinguished European men of letters proclaim the sacred rights of their own nationality: but if one nation has a sacred right to exist, all nations have; and the infringement of a sacred right is a sacrilegious wrong. That wrong is committed by any man of letters who does not raise his voice and hand to prevent one nation from crushing another. There is an allegiance owed to literature.

The world's literature depends for its richness upon diversity; and difference of nationality creates the most interesting diversity. Life and its phenomena do not appear the same to a Russian and a Belgian. Crush Russia, and you maim or bruise her national life, and with her national life her power of utterance, — you crush in the egg Tolstoïs and Dostoievskis still unborn. Destroy Belgium, and you deprive the world's literature of all that which new Maeterlincks would create. No nation can be maimed, without suffering in soul as well as in body. The full functioning of national life is necessary to a fine flowering of literature. Athens produced Æschylus, Euripides, Sophocles, in the time of her glory; England bred Shakspere, Spenser, Hooker, Bacon, in the reign of Queen Elizabeth; Corneille, Racine, Molière, La Fontaine, flourished in the golden days of Louis XIV. Lower a nation's vitality, and her spirit becomes languid; she no longer possesses the living energy to produce what she might otherwise have done.

When a nation is sick, the noblest parts of her suffer first.

A cowed nation cannot bring forth a noble literature. But a little state may have as great a soul as a mighty state; witness the Athens of Pericles, the Florence of Lorenzo de' Medici, or Holland in its great days. No man of letters, unless blinded by ignoble passion, would consent to the national destruction of any state. The rule laid down by Immanuel Kant for the foundation of perpetual peace applies with double force to the lasting prosperity of literature: "No independent State (little or great is in this case all one) shall be capable of becoming the property of another State by inheritance, exchange, purchase, or gift"; and if not by peaceful means, still less by violent means. The Commonwealth of Literature demands that all her constituent parts be respected.

Literatures can help one another; indeed no literature, unaided by another, can attain its fullest development. As each nation prospers best in material things by exchanging commodities with other nations, so each literature prospers best by exchanging commodities of the intellect. The cross-breeding of minds is necessary for new intellectual products. The history of all literatures is full of the benefits derived from one another.   Italy, Spain, England, France, Germany, in their respective flowering seasons, owe much to the achievements of the others.   Literatures are like plants that need pollen wafted from afar in order to bear their brightest blossoms.   The influence of Shakspere, Scott, and Byron, of Montaigne and Rousseau, of Petrarch and Tasso, of Goethe, of Ibsen, of all fertile genius, has been nearly as great in foreign literatures as in their own.   Destroy one nation and you deprive the literatures of all other nations of untold seeds of increase.

The unworthy predicament in which some notable European men of letters stand, is that they have let themselves become so drunk with national egotism that they do not perceive the permanent need which the literature of each nation has of the literature of all other nations, and therefore they have committed high treason against the "Republic of Letters."